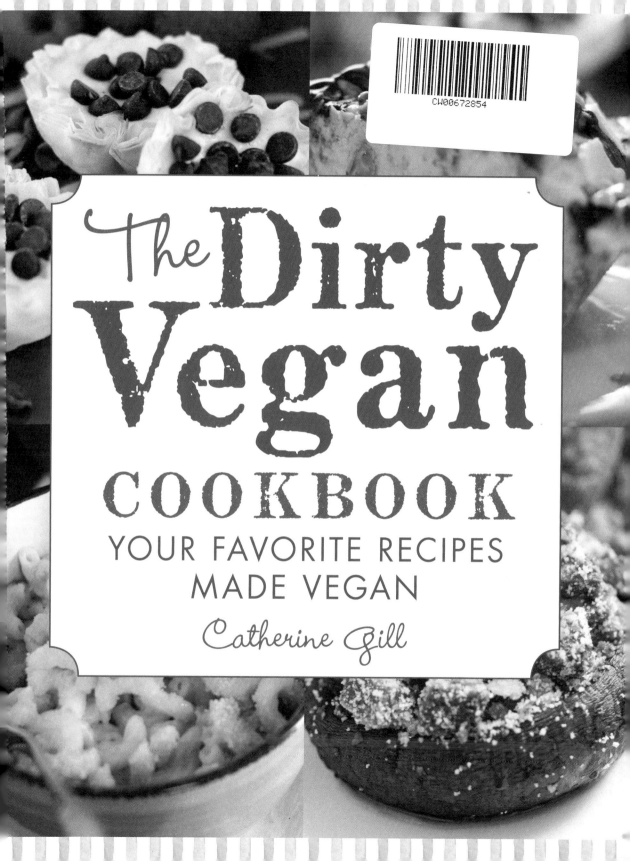

The Dirty Vegan

COOKBOOK

YOUR FAVORITE RECIPES MADE VEGAN

Catherine Gill

Dirty Vegan

Text copyright © 2017 Catherine Gill

Library of Congress Cataloging-in-Publication Data is available upon request.

ISBN: 978-1-578-267-125

Cover and Interior Design by Carolyn Kasper

Printed in the United States

10 9 8 7 6 5 4 3 2

Contents

Recipes

Vegan Ravioli Dippers,
page 37

Foreword

Idream of a world of complete equality—one where there is peace for all beings, including animals. I am confident that in doing so we will create a world free of suffering. This has been my goal for quite some time now, and *The Dirty Vegan Cookbook* is my latest contribution to the cause. The more people choose to eat vegan instead of consuming animal products, the better human health will become, the cleaner the environment will be, and the safer the animals will be from harm.

Whether you are just beginning your journey as a plant-based eater and are planning to add one or two meatless meals to your weekly meal plan, or you are a seasoned vegan eater looking for a great cookbook with new and exciting dishes, this is the cookbook for you. It is my hope that this cookbook will help to make life easier for those who are struggling to find simplicity and balance in veganism. This book outlines the popular products to keep on hand to make vegan cooking free of hassle, and offers simple, easy-to-follow directions to create delicious and practical dishes. You'll soon see that the vegan diet can appeal to everyone!

As a cookbook collector myself, I love the recipes you'll find in gourmet vegan books, but let's face it: they are anything but practical. While I enjoy making exotic or complicated recipes on occasion, making a trip to a specialty food store or two and spending a day or more in preparation, can be exhausting—especially if you're new to the vegan lifestyle.

In writing this cookbook, I wanted to stay away from doing that to you all, completely. This cookbook is free of those scary, complicated-sounding ingredients, and calls only for products that have decent availability in most supermarkets. The recipes in this cookbook are my actual, everyday recipes.

To my readers, so many of whom e-mail me asking what it is I eat every day, and love seeing the photographs of food that I post on social media: this cookbook is for you…and, of course, for the animals.

Peace always,

Catherine

Vegan Dark Chocolate
Peanut Butter Blossoms,
page 182

What is a Dirty Vegan?

Numerous people have asked me why I chose the name, The Dirty Vegan. It's been my official and unofficial title for so many years, it seems natural to me. In fact, it's a nickname that I was using to refer to myself ever since the day I became vegan. Its origins lie in an offhand remark; someone once observed that, since I'm a vegan, that must mean I'm a clean eater. I responded by saying that, although vegan food is much healthier than animal products, my love of rich, indulgent foods means I will always be a Dirty Vegan at heart.

But, you may ask, if that's the case, why be vegan?

The truth is that I've always been this way, even if I didn't know it. But even as a child, I was destined to be an animal rights activist. I can recall myself as young as 4 years old, questioning my parents about animal products, asking about the veins that I would find in chicken or steak, or the blood I'd found in an egg yolk. My mom would tell me, "That's just the way it is; it's part of the animal," but I couldn't accept that.

In fact, I would protest it!

I would argue with my parents and wonder why we had to eat meat, given that we were a family of animal lovers. My dad would just shrug his shoulders, and give me a sympathetic look of pity. He felt the same way as I did; my dad refused to eat anything with a bone in it and never ate steak. Were it not for my mother being an "old-school" Italian, raised by immigrants who had never heard of vegetarianism, ours would have been a vegetarian house for sure.

As I grew older and began making my own meals, I dipped my toe into the world of processed vegetarian products. Boy, were they pretty terrible back then! The taste was something else entirely. When the first vegetarian marketed products hit shelves, they were still a work in progress, but I ate them anyway. By the time I was a teenager, I wasn't eating any red meat at all, but I was still battling an Italian family. In my family's culture, everything is based around food; the only thing more important than the food on the table is the people seated around it. Animal products are used in every aspect

of Italian cooking, and at the time there were hardly any products available that you could substitute into Italian recipes.

Yet even back then, vegetarians were making their own foods—creating cheeses out of nuts, things like that. In fact, a lot of the amazing vegan products we use today had already been invented; they just weren't available in every store yet. Today, any grocery store or superstore with a cold case or a freezer will almost certainly have a ton of vegan products. But back then, vegans were just getting started…and so was I.

When I moved away to college, I quickly grew tired of eating junky dorm food, and would often drive off campus to a grocery store in the city that had a wonderful natural foods section. I had never seen anything like it; certainly a far cry from the small Connecticut town I grew up in! I felt a connection to these natural foods in a way I'd never before experienced, and as time went on, I expanded my shopping list to include as many wholesome food products as possible. My roommate would see me come back to our room with my grocery bags and she could only laugh, asking just what it was I'd bought that day. My only reply was to tell her not to eat any of it. Hey, back then specialty natural products were even more expensive than they are today!

Of course, everything up to this point had been centered around my diet, and a preference for not eating meat. It wasn't until years later, when I received an email from PETA (People for the Ethical Treatment of Animals) that this preference was transformed into an ethos and a lifestyle. The e-mail contained a link to a video, cataloging a series of shocking images that an activist had taken inside of a slaughter facility that supplied a popular food chain.

Never had I felt so *woke* as I did after watching that video. What I was experiencing was the sensation of real, meaningful change. For change and awareness to occur, your comfortable bubble of existence must be burst; you must be shaken awake.

I became a vegetarian in that moment.

After my initial shock, I developed a plan of action. I would become the best vegetarian that I could be, one that will inspire others. In that moment, I felt motivated to become an expert in vegetarianism and animal rights, and was determined to change the minds of everyone on the planet. And I have never lost that passion; it has continued to burn in me like a wildfire ever since.

So I was a vegetarian. Pretty cool, huh? I was walking around with a new pep in my step; I felt lighter, I was happier, I started looking visibly healthier. Things were going great. I joined a sorority in my college and was inspiring other people to become vegetarian. I was leading by example, the way I'd wanted. My fellow classmates saw how vegetarianism had changed my life in a positive way, and they wanted to know more about it. People on campus were even following me around, genuinely interested about becoming a vegetarian. They mentioned how shiny my hair was, how clear my skin was, and how they'd noticed a lot of positive vibes coming from me. Vegetarianism seemed like a new kind of magic. The positive karma was unbelievable (and still is!)

I started to become more involved in animal rights, and became involved with the PETA2 street team. PETA2 is the animal rights subsidiary for teenagers, college students and all the really hip activists (though I might be biased). I became a regular on their forums, helping people with questions about food substitution, and became a popular name in the online group. I also would rack up points in my account by sending letters to politicians, judges and other public officials about animal rights related topics. But it still wasn't enough to satisfy my passion.

One day, when I was sitting at my computer desk in my apartment, I thought to myself, "How can I get more involved? How can I be a big animal rights hero?" I wanted to do much more, and be more of an influential person, but I couldn't think of anything beyond what I was already doing (blogging wasn't a popular thing at the time). I turned around and looked at my animal companions, a pair of goldfish named Romeo and Juliet, my inspiration not to eat fish, and came to a realization.

If, as a vegetarian, I don't eat fish, why was I still eating dairy?

I was almost mad at myself. Dairy is obviously an animal product, so why was I still consuming it? That day I went vegan, and I've never looked back. I became healthier than ever once I adopted the vegan lifestyle. My weight got itself in check, and several of the constant, long-term health problems that I had been battling faded away. Even my seasonal allergies seemed a little better!

I started working in the career world, and my lifestyle inspired my coworkers the same way it had my fellow classmates and sorority sisters in college. People couldn't help but come by my desk at lunchtime to see what I had brought, and I would get daily e-mails from my work friends asking what was in my lunchbox. Coworkers started bringing in vegan dishes of their own to show off while eat lunch with me, which in turn inspired me to make fun and interesting dishes to bring in. Everyone was shocked at the recipes I could veganize; I was making seafood flavors, meatless dishes that tasted like the real thing; to them, I was doing the impossible.

Pretty soon, family, friends and coworkers alike were demanding I tell them my recipes! It was getting overwhelming; I knew I had to find an easier way to get these recipes out to the masses. In retrospect, it seems natural that I would decide to become a blogger. Everyone else was doing it, after all; but I wanted to become an all-round vegan lifestyle blogger, something unusual at the time. But there was plenty to talk about! For example, lots of my friends were curious at how I was able to stay vegan *and* fashionable (where was I finding my vegan leather shoes, they wondered?). My brain was being picked constantly about animal rights and my vegan life, so the only reasonable thing to do was to put it all on my blog and create a helpful resource for those wanting to know how to dive into the vegan world.

The Dirty Vegan was born.

As the blog became popular, I started being approached by famous people who wanted me to create recipes for them, requests which often turned into friendships. I found myself answering e-mail questions left and right from readers who were becoming vegan because they'd stumbled across my blog. I heard countless stories about families going meatless and telling me how the whole bunch loves my recipes. I was, and still am incredibly humbled and honored by this. It is so exciting to realize how many animals are being saved by this domino chain of vegans. Me, my readers, their friends, friends of their friends…it seemed like the whole world is going vegan. My plan was working!

Since the blog was a success and my readers were so responsive, I decided to open my own vegan bakery. I started veganizing the things that I missed the most:

classic, retro-inspired snack food desserts. Snack cakes with fluffy white filling, donuts, whoopie pies and many more had been sadly out of reach for those living the vegan lifestyle…until now! Made vegan by me and sold at farmers markets and festivals, the customers were flocking to these new cruelty-free confections. There were even people who came from states away, who followed my blog and wanted to enjoy what my Dirty Vegan Foods bakery stand had to offer. It was unbelievably awesome. And what was even better was all the skeptical non-vegans who became believers after trying our baked goods. We were able to convert so many folks, who were adamant that they'd never like vegan foods, into lovers and loyal customers after just one taste of our free samples!

Dirty Vegan Foods grew out of control. Whole Foods stores wanted our vegan sweets; natural foods markets and grocery stores ordered from us; business was certainly booming. Whole Foods quickly went from having Dirty Vegan Foods in major stores in New England to wanting us on the entire East Coast! The only problem was, since we were such a small operation, we were receiving orders we had to struggle to fill. Between online sales, farmers markets and festivals, and store orders to stock, we were overwhelmed, but weren't making enough money to cover costs *and* hire new help.

It was around this time that I became pregnant, and soon developed complications that led my doctor to recommend I take a break from Dirty Vegan Foods. It *is* still there, and everything is still trademarked; but sadly, we're not up and running anymore. There remains a cult following for Dirty Vegan Foods, with Facebook and Twitter followers asking regularly when we will be available again. And it will be back one day, I promise! Everything happens for a reason and in its own moment, when the time is right. I have no doubt that there will be a Dirty Vegan Foods bakery storefront or diner again someday.

For now, I am happy to share with you everything that that name stands for, along with all the passion, wisdom and experience I have earned in the years I spent transforming my nickname into a phenomenon.

Sicilian Pizza, page 43

What Makes This Book Special?

✳

The recipes that comprise this book are intended to capture the *true* essence of what it means to be a dirty vegan.

But what does that mean?

Well, it means that nowhere in this cookbook will you find any boring "diet food" recipes. While there are some vegans that restrict themselves to healthy, raw superfoods only, I like making a variety of dishes drawn from different styles of cuisine. How can I do this and still stay completely vegan?

Well, the truth is this: you can "veganize" *anything*—no recipe is too challenging! That means you *can* enjoy delicious cheesiness or candy goodness, you *can* enjoy milkshakes, you *can* enjoy any of the foods that you may have previously thought "off limits" to a vegan.

I've heard feedback from so many people since becoming vegan, learning what people miss, what people crave, and what others have tried to make vegan but failed. With years of working as a vegan chef under my belt and a long, happy history of life without animal products, I've been able to put together this book and take the guesswork out of vegan cooking. The hard part's over!

What do I mean when I say guesswork? I ran into a friend from high school the other day, and as we got to catching up, talking about my activism and lifestyle, she mentioned that she'd tried desperately to cook vegan food, but with no luck; she said that the result tasted awful. I politely asked her for an example of something she'd made, and she described a veggie ground "beef" she'd made, to go with a pasta dish. When I asked her how she'd prepared it, she told me that she'd just thrown it in the pan—no oil or seasonings.

The moral of the story—and the secret to this cookbook—is this: you must treat vegan products exactly as you would treat non-vegan products. You still need to oil the pan, add in flavorful ingredients, and season foods with those spices that will best express their flavors. All foods must be seasoned properly in order achieve a decent taste, much less chef quality or gourmet results.

The recipes in this cookbook will get you into the habit of preparing and seasoning vegan food to perfection. I can promise that you'll be wowing anyone you cook for—these recipes are certainly not lacking in the flavor department. When I first began experimenting with vegan cuisine, I kept two principles in mind. First: what ingredients should I substitute in order to remove the animal products and make the recipe vegan? Second: what ingredients must I use to make the recipe work the way I want it to? What should I use as a binder instead of egg? How do I achieve this texture or that aftertaste?

What makes my cookbook unique is that I take on the recipes that most people don't expect *can* be made vegan. But it's more than that. I take dishes that have already been veganized, and I do them the Dirty Vegan way—no compromises to taste, no "diet" foods obsessions, no impossible-to-find ingredients. (Nothing is worse than buying a great cookbook and then not being able to use it because you'd need to go halfway 'round the world to track down the ingredients it calls for.)

I believe in developing recipes that are as effortless as they can possibly be, with simplified ingredients and smarter techniques. People often tell me that following my recipes is such a breeze, and I couldn't be happier. Cooking should always be enjoyable and never a burden.

Now, let's have some fun!

The Vegan Pantry Guide

✳

Here are my vegan pantry recommendations, though you can feel free to customize this list to suit your needs. The ingredients listed in this section are the staples that I like to have in my pantry to ensure I can prepare (or invent) a variety of different meals. They also constitute the bulk of the ingredients needed to prepare all the recipes in this cookbook! These items make life as a vegan so simple that you'll be able to veganize practically anything; not to mention, having these on hand makes it easier to prepare specialty recipes—you only need to run out and buy a few key ingredients!

This list is not exhaustive—in fact, there are probably items that I have missed—but it is a good "starter" checklist of items for any vegan to have.

Baking powder: Used in many baked goods and other recipes and vital to have on hand in your cupboard.

Baking soda: Used in many baked goods and other recipes and vital to have on hand in your cupboard. Baking soda can also be used in recipes to reduce their acidity (I have used this method in making tomato marinara sauce).

Bacon bits: A staple in my pantry, bacon bits add a nice "meaty" and smoky flavor to dishes. You can find traditional brands that carry a vegan version, or you can try the many organic and natural bacon bits that are marketed as vegan.

Beans: I like to keep canned and dry beans on hand at all times; when opting for the canned variety I prefer natural, organic, BPA and preservative-free. Some canned beans that I always have in my cupboard include: cannellini, kidney, black, garbanzo, navy and pinto. (I will also grab other kinds like fava, mung or others when I see them on sale!)

Black pepper: I use ground black pepper in almost everything that I make. I prefer buying black peppercorns and adding them to my pepper grinder; it makes for a fresher peppery taste. However, purchasing pre-ground pepper is great, too; do whatever is suits your budget or your particular preference.

Black salt powder: This ingredient is a pantry staple if you want to make your vegan foods taste more like the real thing. Black salt powder tastes very much like eggs due to a strong sulfur flavor, so it enhances anything vegan recipe that mimics eggs.

Butter: All good chefs put butter in pretty much anything they can get away with, so I recommend finding a good vegan butter or buttery spread that you really love, and always keep it on hand.

Cheeses: I always have a variety of vegan cheeses on hand, including grated parmesan, shredded cheddar and mozzarella, and blocks of various flavors (as well as vegan cheese slices in multiple flavors). There are only a few recipes in this cookbook that call for specialty cheese flavors—mostly shredded cheddar or mozzarella—which is available in most grocery stores.

Chia seeds: Chia is a superfood that contains omega-3 fatty acids and is known for having various health benefits. What's more, it can actually be used as a vegan egg replacement! When you soak chia seeds in a little bit of water, it creates a gel-like paste that acts as an effective binder. You can also add chia to smoothies for a nutritional boost.

Coconut oil: This is something that I always have in my pantry. I like to invest in good quality organic coconut oil, but this is not strictly necessary. Coconut oil has recently enjoyed a surge in popularity, and is now being carried in most grocery stores.

Corn starch: Corn starch is a wonderful ingredient to have handy in your cupboard, which I use primarily to thicken sauces.

Cream cheese: Vegan cream cheese is a staple in my house, and can be used for anything from spreading on bagels to making sauces cheesier, and is always wonderful when used in dip recipes.

Crescent roll dough: A good quality can of crescent rolls is really useful to have around the house, and it should come as no surprise that it is featured in almost every section of this cookbook! Make sure to read the package to ensure that it *is* in fact vegan-friendly; I prefer the more natural or organic offerings, which have only been getting easier to find.

Edamame: Another name for an immature soy bean, harvested prior to becoming hardened, edamame can be boiled or steamed, and seasoned or just sprinkled with some salt. High in protein, they make a wonderful and healthful snack, as well as an excellent addition to your recipes. You can find edamame shelled or in the pod, fresh or frozen.

Egg replacer: Egg replacers include commercial powders that you mix with water as well as items like ground flaxseed or chia seed. I like to keep a commercial egg replacer on hand in my kitchen cabinet, though there are any number of options available when looking to replace eggs in your recipes, including tofu, banana, applesauce, beans, mashed potato, chia, flax…the list goes on! It all depends on what you're making; that's why I say to experiment with vegan cooking (and keep practicing!)

Extracts: I like having a variety of extracts on hand, the most important of which is pure vanilla. If you find that you have run out of vanilla extract, and are making something that also calls for vegan milk, I find that you can use vanilla flavored milk or coffee creamer when in a pinch.

Flaxseed: High in fiber and containing omega-3 fatty acids, flaxseed makes for a very healthy addition to one's diet (and is very cost effective). I mostly buy this ingredient in its ground form, and I use it mainly as an egg replacer. I'll usually get a one pound bag; once opened, I store it in my refrigerator in an airtight container, labeled with the date it was opened. Compared to the amount of money one dozen eggs costs (and that the speed at which they spoil), it's easy to see that flaxseed is superior. You can get a lot of vegan "eggs" from that inexpensive bag of ground flaxseed! I will also added flaxseed to smoothies to give them a little boost.

Flour: I like to keep a few different types of flours in my pantry, including whole wheat, almond, coconut and garbanzo flours. That said, the one type of flour that I always have in my cupboard is all-purpose flour; I prefer a decent quality all-purpose flour, one that is unbleached and unbromated. Make sure to read the back of the packaging to confirm that it is substantial and not empty calorie. The flour should contain protein and fat, and be higher in calories than bleached flour.

Garlic: Fresh garlic is a must for flavor enhancing in any cooking, and especially in vegan cooking. A dash of garlic makes a boring tofu fillet taste amazing! It brings such a strong yet pleasant taste to food, and is said to have some amazing health benefits. I alternate between buying the fresh cloves and the pre-minced garlic in the jar.

Garlic powder: I use garlic powder a lot in my recipes. It enhances flavor beautifully without overpowering the other flavors, and has a much longer shelf life than fresh garlic. When you want garlic flavor and fresh garlic is not a must, garlic powder is a great choice. I also find that garlic powder makes tofu taste phenomenal.

Hummus: Hummus is a staple in many a vegan's refrigerator. You can add hummus to many recipes to make them creamier, use it as a dip, a salad enhancer...there are so many possibilities with hummus! If you are a first time vegan, or trying to go vegan, hummus is a great food item to have stocked at all times.

Ketchup: I always use organic and natural ketchup; make sure to store it in the refrigerator and *not* in the cupboard—regardless of what the label says!

Lemon: I use fresh lemon juice in so many dishes—even adding fresh lemon to my drinking water—that fresh lemons are a fixture in my home. If you decide to use all-natural lemon juice in a glass bottle, pay attention to the expiration date on the bottle and how long it will stay fresh.

Lentils: Keeping a bag or two of dried lentils is a great idea in a vegan household. Lentils are a fiber and protein powerhouse—16 grams of fiber and 18 grams of protein per 1 cup cooked lentils! You can do a lot with lentils, and storing dried lentils couldn't be easier; if stored properly, lentils will keep in your cupboard without spoilage for one full year!

Liquid aminos: With a taste like soy sauce and able to be used as such, most liquid amino products are free of preservatives and added salt content. The liquid amino brand that I buy contains 15 essential amino acids, which I feel is important for vegans and non-vegans alike to include in their diets.

Maple syrup: You will notice recipes in this cookbook calling for maple syrup quite often. I use pure maple syrup as an alternative to sugar or sweetener because it blends in so nicely.

Mayonnaise: Vegan mayonnaise is, without exaggeration, my best friend. Vital in vegan cuisine, vegan mayonnaise makes vegan food creamy and flavorful, while adding oil in a subtle and tasty way. Read the labels on the back on vegan mayonnaises and choose the one that is right for you based on ingredients and your flavor preference.

Meats: I stock up my refrigerator and freezer the same way a non-vegan would. In addition to tofu, beans, lentil and other proteins, I like to have a variety of vegan meats like "chicken", "beef", "seafood" and whatever others I can find. I personally like to have a diverse choice of vegan meats on hand, so that I'm prepared to make any dish I desire.

Mustards: I like to keep dry mustard, prepared yellow mustard and Dijon mustard on hand. You can use mustard in so many recipes and in lots of different ways, so it is an important (not to mention flavorful) condiment to have in the kitchen.

Noodles: Udon, soba, angel hair pasta, ramen, rice and so many other vegan noodles inspire so many extraordinary dishes—so long as you actually have them in your pantry. Pay attention to the expiration dates and don't keep so many that you can't use them before they expire.

Nuts: You just *have* to have some nuts in the pantry. I like almonds, cashews, peanuts and walnuts best. Packed with protein and both monounsaturated and polyunsaturated fats, nuts are a go-to for vegans and all other humans (so long as they're not allergic!)

Nut and seed butters: There are so many nut and seed butters out there these days that it can be absolutely overwhelming. I like to keep a few on my shelf or in my refrigerator at home, switching up the styles when I care to. I find that peanut butter, almond butter, sunflower seed butter and cashew butter work best, and keep them consistently stocked in my kitchen.

Nutritional yeast: Nutritional yeast (also known to many vegans by the nickname "nooch") is deactivated yeast, which has a cheesy and nutty flavor. But making your vegan food taste like cheese isn't the only trick up nooch's sleeve; one serving of nooch contains 9 grams of "perfect" protein, meaning that it contains all 9 amino acids that the human body is unable to produce. Nutritional yeast also offers other health benefits, including decent amounts of iron and B vitamins (depending on whether it is unfortified or fortified).

Olive oil: Olive oil is like liquid gold in my home. I choose extra-virgin olive oil for most food preparation; however, feel free to use whichever variety you prefer.

Onions: Fresh onion can be the determining factor between dish that is merely "good" one that tastes *amazing*. Onions come in different varieties that have differences in flavor, so experiment with the onions that you use in your meals.

Onion powder: I like to use onion powder when I'm looking to add onion flavoring to a dish but don't feel like cutting up onions, or when pieces of onion would negatively affect the texture or "look" of a recipe.

Pastas: Most people don't realize that a typical serving of quality cooked pasta contains an average of 9 grams of protein! I've been known to go a little overboard in the pasta aisle. Being an Italian-American, I love my pasta; I am a fan of all vegan varieties, but my favorites to keep in the cupboard are lasagna, spaghetti, shells, elbows, orzo, ziti and rotini.

Produce: I keep well-stocked produce bins, changing things up weekly or seasonally. Variety is key with fresh fruits and vegetables; look to eat the colors of the rainbow and then some, when it comes to your fruit and veggie intake!

Rice: There are a wide variety of rice types available. I always have brown, white, basmati, jasmine and wild rice in regular rotation in my kitchen.

Salt: Any salt will do just fine, though I prefer fine sea salt or Himalayan pink salt.

Seasonings: A well-stocked spice rack is very important—well, it is to me at least!

Seaweed: Seaweeds like nori are available in many different preparations; my favorite to keep stocked is nori sheets or flakes. You can find this in the specialty foods aisle of any grocery store or where sushi ingredients are sold. Adding nori and other edible seaweeds will bring an ocean of flavor to your foods, especially when making mock seafood dishes.

Soy sauce: A wonderful flavor enhancer for many types of recipes; make sure to opt for the lower sodium styles if you're sensitive to salt.

Seeds: Seeds, like sunflower, pumpkin, sesame and so many others, can really upgrade your meals.

Sugars: I like to keep vegan and organic cane sugar, as well as coconut, powdered, light brown and dark brown sugars to give me a good variety to work with. There are plenty of new and exciting vegan sugars and sweetener options out there these days, so find what works best for you.

Tempeh: Tempeh is a soybean product that is slightly less processed than tofu and contains a respectable amount of protein (31 grams per serving!) and fiber content, in addition to calcium, iron, vitamin B-6, magnesium and potassium. Tempeh can be used in stir-fry recipes, sliced and made into vegan bacon, and used in countless recipes.

Tofu: I always keep tofu in my refrigerator, usually the firm or extra firm variety, because I find that it is among the most versatile ingredients a vegan can stock. You can prepare it firm or use it blended, mashed, crumbled, et cetera, without any problem.

Tomato paste: Canned tomato paste is an easy product to keep in your pantry and can be used in various recipes and dishes.

Tomato sauce: When you are pressed for time, jarred tomato marinara sauce is just the right kind of convenient. I prefer the natural varieties and flavors and use them whenever I don't have time to make my own tomato sauce.

Vegetable broth and stock: A staple in any vegan pantry, vegetable broth and stock are used in so many recipes that you really can't afford to go without!

Worcestershire sauce: This condiment is used in "meat" dishes, dips and a lot of other preparations. Ensure the kind that you choose does not contain animal products and says "vegan" right on the label (non-vegan Worcestershire sauce will contain anchovies).

The Recipes

Bacon Jalapeno Bites,
page 105

Snacks and Appetizers

This section is for those moments when you want something a little substantial, but not as filling as a full meal. These recipes are ideal for when you need a little something to get you through until dinner, or if you need some nourishing hors d'oeuvres to put out when entertaining guests.

Lasagna Rolls

Makes 12 rolls

What I love about this dish is the way it lets you enjoy lasagna in an easy appetizer form, no cutting required. An excellent choice to serve at cocktail parties or anytime you are expecting company, this is one of my go-to appetizer recipes when I am entertaining guests.

12 lasagna noodles
1 (14-ounce) block firm tofu, drained
4 ounces vegan cream cheese
1 tablespoon extra-virgin olive oil
1 teaspoon dried Italian seasoning
½ teaspoon onion powder
¼ teaspoon garlic powder

Pinch of salt
Pinch of pepper
24 ounces pasta marinara sauce
1 cup vegan mozzarella cheese, shredded
2 tablespoons extra-virgin olive oil, divided

Preheat oven to 350°F. In a large pot, boil water and cool lasagna noodles until tender; drain and set aside.

Place tofu, cream, cheese, olive oil and seasonings in blender and puree until smooth. Take about ¼ cup of marinara sauce plus 1 tablespoon of olive oil and spread on bottom of a 9 x 13-inch baking dish. Once cool enough to handle, take each lasagna noodle and add a small amount of tofu mixture. Roll it up to cover it, add another dollop of tofu mixture on the overhanging noodle and roll, before placing the lasagna roll in the baking dish seam-side down.

Once all 12 rolls are completed, pour the remaining marinara sauce on top. Sprinkle with shredded mozzarella and drizzle 1 tablespoon of olive oil on top on cheese. Bake uncovered for 30–40 minutes or until cheese is melted. Let sit for about 10 minutes to set before serving.

Maple "Bacon" Cheddar Stuffed Sweet Potato

Makes 8 stuffed halves

There is something special about the way the flavors of sweet potato and maple syrup coordinate with smoky "bacon" and cheddar cheese. This recipe perfectly demonstrates this phenomenon!

4 large sweet potatoes
2 tablespoons vegan butter
2 tablespoons vegan bacon bits
2 tablespoons maple syrup
¾ cup vegan cheddar cheese, shredded

4 tablespoons vegan sour cream
2 tablespoons fresh parsley, chopped
Salt and pepper, to taste

Wash sweet potatoes. Poke holes in sweet potatoes and microwave them for 6–9 minutes (or use your microwave oven's potato setting) or until tender. Allow to cool enough to handle safely, then slice potatoes in half lengthwise. Scoop out middles of sweet potatoes and reserve. Place the outer portion of potatoes and set on a greased baking sheet.

In a food processor, blend sweet potato middles, butter, salt and pepper. Remove; in a mixing bowl, fold in bacon bits and maple syrup. Spoon mixture into sweet potato shells, top with cheddar cheese and broil on high for 10 minutes or until cheese is melted. Top with sour cream and parsley.

Stuffed Zucchini Boat Bites

Makes 12 bites

An ideal recipe to keep in mind for those farmers' market trips, these bites make for fun "finger foods" at any cocktail party, gathering, holiday or cookout.

3 medium zucchini, yellow or green	¼ cup vegan mozzarella cheese, shredded
1 large red bell pepper, finely chopped	1 tablespoon vegan parmesan cheese, grated
½ cup and 3 tablespoons panko break crumbs	1 tablespoon vegan bacon bits
½ cup vegan cream cheese	1 tablespoon extra-virgin olive oil
1 tablespoon Dijon mustard	Salt and pepper, to taste

Wash zucchini and cut off stems. Cut zucchini in half lengthwise, then in half at the center. Scoop the middle out of zucchini pieces to make small "boats" and room for stuffing; arrange them on a greased baking sheet.

In a mixing bowl, combine chopped bell pepper, ½ cup panko bread crumbs, cream cheese, mustard, mozzarella, parmesan, "bacon" bits, salt and pepper. Stuff boats with stuffing and top with remaining 3 tablespoons bread crumbs. Drizzle with olive oil and broil on high for 10 minutes or until zucchini is slightly tender and tops are golden brown.

Eric Schiffer's Fresh and Toasty Summer Bruschetta Bites

Makes 2 dozen

Eric Schiffer is well-known for being a bestselling author, an entrepreneur, a business expert, and a member of Mensa—among many other achievements (he's also the CEO of Patriarch.org). You have probably seen his famous face on television; he is a frequent correspondent on CNN, FOX, CNBC, and MSNBC.

On top of all of his notable accomplishments, Eric is also a vegan and animal rights activist. Since Eric and his celebrity girlfriend, Dr. Jenn Mann, frequent a popular vegan restaurant in Los Angeles that specializes in Mediterranean small dishes, I wanted to create this appetizer for him—perfect for when the fabulous couple wants that restaurant dish but have decided to dine at home. With a combination of toasty bread and fresh flavors on top, all while being super convenient to prepare, this is a deal-making recipe for any lively jet-setter. You can follow Eric on Twitter @EricSchiffer.

---

1 large baguette bread loaf, sliced evenly into 24 pieces
¼ cup vegan butter, melted
8 ripe plum tomatoes, chopped
1 garlic clove, minced
1 tablespoon balsamic vinegar

2½ teaspoons extra-virgin olive oil
½ teaspoon onion powder
1 teaspoon sugar
2 tablespoons fresh basil, chopped
Salt and pepper, to taste

Preheat oven to 450°F and arrange bread slices evenly on two ungreased baking sheets. Brush bread with melted butter and bake for 5–8 minutes, or until toasted.

In a large mixing bowl, combine tomatoes, garlic, vinegar, olive oil, onion powder, sugar, basil, salt and pepper to taste; mix until thoroughly combined. Arrange toasted bread slices on a serving platter with tomato mixture spooned on top. Alternatively, you can serve tomato mixture in a bow with a serving spoon in it, alongside toasted bread in a basket.

Mini Cheese Balls

Makes 24 mini cheese balls

Many vegans have told me that cheese balls are something that they have trouble making vegan. I made this recipe to change that!

1 (8-ounce) container vegan cream cheese
2 tablespoons vegan butter
1 cup vegan cheddar cheese, shredded

1 cup blanched almonds, finely chopped
24 thin pretzel sticks

With an electric mixer, beat cream cheese and butter until well combined and fluffy. Fold in cheddar cheese.

Roll into 24 balls that are about 1 tablespoon in size. Roll each cheese ball into chopped almonds and refrigerate for at least 30 minutes to 1 hour. Before serving, press a pretzel stick into the top middle of each cheese ball.

Devilled Tofu Bites

Makes 6–8 servings

If you serve these tofu bites at your next party, be prepared to accept a *lot* of compliments! Everyone that eats one will be proclaiming, "These taste just like devilled eggs!" (Just be sure to smile and say thank you!)

1 (15-ounce) block firm tofu, drained	Ground black pepper, to taste
½ ripe avocado, peeled and pitted	Black salt powder, to taste
¼ cup vegan mayonnaise	Ground paprika, to taste

On a cutting board, slice tofu block in half lengthwise. Cut each half down the middle lengthwise, giving you four evenly sized pieces. Cut each tofu strip into four, giving you 16 small rectangles in total. Arrange 16 tofu pieces on a serving platter.

In a food processor or blender, combine avocado and mayonnaise; season with black pepper and black salt powder, to taste. Spread evenly on each tofu piece or use a piping bag to pipe filling on. Sprinkle paprika on top of tofu bites, to taste. Refrigerate until ready to serve.

Boneless Buffalo Style "Wings" with Blue Cheese Dipping Sauce

Makes 10 boneless wings

Once I figured out how to make these and was able to get the flavors right, I couldn't stop eating them! (I am *not* kidding; there was a point when I was making these every single day.) When you make something vegan that you haven't had in many years, it is really exciting stuff. Even before I went vegan, I only liked the flavors of the buffalo sauce and the cool creamy dip (as opposed to the chicken's flavor). Once I made the recipe vegan, I wondered why I hadn't done it sooner! It's okay; better late than never.

---

10 vegan chicken tenders or nuggets
⅛–¼ cup hot cayenne pepper sauce (depending on your heat preference)
⅛–¼ cup vegan butter (do a 1:1 ratio with however much hot sauce you choose)
2 tablespoon vegan mayonnaise
2 tablespoons vegan cream cheese
¼ cup of vegan parmesan cheese, grated
1 teaspoon Dijon mustard
1 teaspoon fresh lemon juice
2 large celery stalks, cut into sticks, for garnish (optional)
1 large carrot, cut into sticks, for garnish (optional)
Salt, to taste

Prepare the vegan tenders or nuggets according to package directions.

In a small saucepan, melt the vegan butter, then whisk in hot sauce and set aside.

In a small mixing bowl, combine mayonnaise, cream cheese, parmesan, mustard, lemon juice and salt; transfer to a small serving bowl or dip bowl.

When tenders or nuggets are ready, transfer them to a large mixing bowl and toss in buffalo sauce mixture; transfer to a serving dish along with cheese dip bowl and garnish plate with celery and carrots. Serve immediately.

Avocado and "Bacon" Cheesy Cheddar Bread Ring

Serves 6–8

There are no specific size guidelines to follow when making this bread ring. If you like a thinner crust, roll out the dough thinner and make a bigger circle. If you prefer thicker crust and a "breadier" taste, keep the circle small. Just remember that the thickness will dictate cooking time: a thicker bread ring will take a little longer to cook than a thinner one.

¼ all-purpose flour (for baking sheet and bread rolling)
16 ounces prepared pizza dough
¼ cup vegan cream cheese
1 tablespoon Dijon mustard
1 tablespoon maple syrup
1 large ripe avocado, peeled and pitted

1 (5.5-ounce) package vegan bacon, chopped
1 cup vegan cheddar cheese, shredded
1 tablespoon olive oil
½ teaspoon dried parsley flakes (optional)

Preheat oven to 400°F and line a baking sheet with high temperature resistant parchment paper. Sprinkle a small amount of flour on the baking sheet.

On a floured surface, roll out dough to a large, thin circular shape. Place on baking sheet and with a pizza cutter, slice a line about 2 inches long in the middle of the circle, then another in the middle of that line to make an "X", then once more to make a "star".

In a bowl, mix cream cheese, mustard and maple syrup; spread evenly on ring. Slice avocado and arrange around dough ring, topping with "bacon" and cheese. Take the dough from the middle and wrap it around to the outer edge of the ring until it forms a "stuffed" ring appearance. With olive oil, brush top of dough and drizzle over exposed cheese.

Bake for 20–30 minutes or until dough is cooked thoroughly, bread ring is golden brown and cheese is melty. Allow to set for easier cutting and serving. Cut into slices. Enjoy bread "as-is" or with your favorite dipping sauce.

Creamy Avocado Dip

Serves 4–6

I don't know many people who don't like a good avocado dip. This is an awesome dip to make for any occasion, whether it be just to hang around the house and watch movies or to take along with you the next time you are invited to a gathering. Don't worry, I'll let you take the credit on this one!

2 ripe avocados	¼ teaspoon onion powder
1 tablespoon fresh lemon juice	⅛ teaspoon garlic powder
1 (8-ounce) container vegan cream cheese	Salt, to taste

Peel and remove the pit from avocadoes.

In a medium bowl, mash avocado together with lemon juice then mix in remaining ingredients. Serve with chips, raw vegetables, crackers or bread.

Vegan Ravioli Dippers

Makes 30 ravioli dippers

Unless you are a professional pasta maker, getting your hands on vegan ravioli is not going to happen. I have only seen one or two brands that sell frozen vegan ravioli, and even then only at select natural foods grocery chains. What's more, you can't always find ravioli wrappers in the pasta aisle of your average grocery store, while in the specialty Italian markets, most ravioli pasta contain egg or dairy.

Given that I don't always have time to make homemade pasta, I've always dreamed of an easier option. Then, as I was making lasagna rolotinis one night, the pastas were sticking together because of the style I'd chosen to use. That evening while I was asleep, I had a dream about using those same problematic noodles to make ravioli, and it worked! I tried it out the next day, and it worked in real life, too!

This recipe takes things one step further by making it into a fun crispy appetizer. These can be prepared as ravioli pasta with marinara sauce, as long as you crimp seal the outer edges properly and boil them.

10 no-boil/oven ready lasagna noodle sheets (must be flat and smooth, not the wavy or ridged kind)	1 teaspoon dried Italian seasoning
	¼ teaspoon onion powder
	¼ teaspoon garlic powder
1 (15-ounce) block firm tofu, well-drained	1 "egg" equivalent, vegan egg replacer
¼ cup vegan parmesan cheese, grated	2 tablespoons vegan butter, melted
	1 cup bread crumbs
¼ cup vegan mozzarella cheese, shredded	Olive oil cooking spray
	1 cup tomato marinara sauce
2 tablespoons vegan cream cheese	Salt and pepper, to taste

Preheat oven to 400°F and line two baking sheets with high temperature resistant parchment paper. Boil lasagna noodles in water for 7–10 minutes, or until they look soft and easy to work with. Spray the baking sheets lightly with olive oil cooking spray.

In a large mixing bowl, mash tofu with a fork, and then mix in parmesan, mozzarella, cream cheese, Italian seasoning, onion powder, garlic powder, salt and pepper to taste; mix until well-combined.

Drain lasagna water and quickly replace with cool water (if noodles are left without water, they will stick together fast and be difficult to work with). Spray a cutting board with olive oil spray. Working quickly, because lasagna gets sticky quickly, pick up one noodle once it is cool enough to handle, lay it down on cutting board, and dollop three tablespoons of tofu cheese filling, one tablespoon at a time, in the middle. Make sure the dollops are evenly spread apart, like the three lights in a stop light. Take another lasagna noodle and gently lay it on top and gently press it down. Spray a pizza cutter with olive oil spray and make two cuts, separating it into three raviolis. They will look like little square pasta sandwiches. Using a pastry crimper or fork, crimp edges of raviolis on all sides to seal them.

In a medium mixing bowl, mix egg replacer according to package directions and whisk in butter. Dunk each stuffed ravioli into "egg" and butter mixture, then dip in breadcrumbs to coat, and place on baking sheet. When all raviolis are stuffed and breaded, spray the tops with olive oil spray. Bake for 20 minutes, or until raviolis are toasted, crispy, and the breading is golden. Serve with warmed marinara sauce for dipping.

"Seafood" Dip

Serves 8

I remember my mother making a dip similar to this when I was growing up, for every New Year's Eve party she hosted. When I turned vegan, I was eager to veganize her recipe—and even more excited once I'd managed to make it taste exactly like I recollected.

1 (8-ounce) container vegan cream cheese
¼ cup onion, minced
⅛ teaspoon garlic powder
½ cup vegan fishless, cooked and chopped

1 sheet nori, crumpled into small pieces or flakes
½ cup cocktail sauce
Salt and pepper, to taste

In a large bowl, mix together cream cheese, onion, garlic powder, fishless, nori, salt and pepper. Transfer dip to serving bowl or plate and refrigerate for at least 1 hour. Just prior to serving, pour cocktail sauce over top of dip and spread evenly. Serve with crackers.

Slow Cooker Spinach and Artichoke Dip

Makes 8–10 servings

This recipe is just so easy! I make this ahead of time whenever I am hosting people at my house, timing it so that it is ready when my guests arrive. It is so simple; just throw a bunch of stuff in a slow cooker, giving it a stir occasionally, and you've got a scrumptious warm dip ready for when your friends walk through the door. One year when I made this during a holiday, my friend thanked me for making her something non-vegan. I had to laugh as I told her it was totally vegan; she was in disbelief, proclaiming it the best spinach and artichoke dip she had ever tasted!

1 (16-ounce) bag frozen chopped spinach
1 (14-ounce) can artichoke hearts, drained and chopped
1 (8-ounce) container vegan cream cheese
½ cup plain vegan milk
1 tablespoon vegan butter

2 cups vegan mozzarella cheese, shredded
¼ cup vegan parmesan cheese, grated
1 teaspoon onion powder
¼ teaspoon garlic powder
Salt and pepper, to taste

Grease the crock of a large slow cooker. In a large mixing bowl, combine spinach, artichoke hearts, cream cheese, milk, butter, cheeses, onion powder, garlic powder, salt and pepper to taste; transfer to slow cooker and cover with lid. Cook for 3 hours on high heat or 4–5 hours on low heat, stirring occasionally. Serve with crackers, chips or slices of baguette bread.

Bacon Jalapeno Bites

Makes 1 dozen bites

These bites are like jalapeno poppers, but better. Super easy to make, they make for a perfect game day recipe, party recipe, or something to make any time you are looking for a great crowd pleasing snack or appetizer.

6 jalapeno peppers, cut in half lengthwise with seeds, stems and inners removed	¾ cup vegan cream cheese 12 strips of your favorite vegan bacon

Preheat oven to 400°F. Lightly grease a baking sheet. Spread 1 tablespoon of cream cheese into each pepper half. Wrap each with a strip of "bacon" and place them on the baking sheet. Bake for 20 minutes.

My Famous Stuffed Portobello Mushroom Caps

Makes 3 stuffed caps

Over the years, these mushrooms have become so popular within my circle of family and friends that I am practically begged to make them for each and every holiday or get-together. In fact, I'm beginning to think that people invite me over just to get these stuffed mushroom caps! I'm certain this recipe will be a hit amongst your circle as well.

3 large Portobello mushroom caps
3 tablespoons extra-virgin olive oil
1 garlic clove, minced
¼ cup onion, finely chopped
2 tablespoons red bell pepper, finely chopped
⅛ cup celery, finely chopped

12 ounces vegan sausage, chopped
⅓ cup breadcrumbs
2 tablespoons vegan parmesan cheese, grated
2 tablespoons fresh parsley, chopped
1 tablespoon balsamic vinegar

Preheat oven to 400°F. Wash Portobello caps and remove stems; reserve stems and chop them finely. Rub mushroom caps with 1 tablespoon of olive oil and place on a greased baking sheet, stem-side up.

In a large skillet on medium heat, sauté garlic and onion in olive oil until fragrant. Add reserved mushroom stems, bell pepper and celery, and sauté until tender. Add sausage and cook until brown. Remove from heat and mix in breadcrumbs, parmesan cheese and parsley; divide mixture into Portobello caps and stuff them. Bake for about 15–20 minutes or until tender and tops are golden brown. Drizzle with balsamic vinegar.

Fondue Dip with French Bread

Serves 4–6

Here's another recipe that a lot of people think cannot be properly done vegan. Fondue most certainly can be done right sans animal products—and here's the proof!

12 ounces beer
1 cup vegan cheddar cheese, shredded
1 cup other style vegan cheese (like mozzarella or Swiss style), shredded

2 tablespoons all-purpose flour
½ teaspoon garlic powder
1 loaf of French bread, cut into cubes
Salt and pepper, to taste

In a saucepan on very low heat, warm beer and gradually add cheeses, flour and garlic powder while stirring constantly until cheeses are melted and dip is well-combined. Season with salt and pepper to taste. Serve immediately with French bread cubes for dipping.

"Bacon" Parmesan Twists with Sweet Dijon Dipping Sauce

Makes 12 twists

When I first turned vegan, I never imagined that creating vegan versions of food that I enjoyed in my childhood would be as easy as it is now! With today's wide variety of vegan products, this recipe can be made with ease by visiting practically any supermarket. These twists will also fool your non-vegan friends; I know firsthand!

Twists
16 ounces prepared pizza dough, divided into 12 pieces
12 slices of vegan bacon
½ cup vegan parmesan cheese, grated

Sauce
2 tablespoons vegan mayonnaise
2 teaspoons Dijon mustard
1 tablespoon maple syrup

Preheat oven to 425°F. On a lightly floured surface, roll out dough to form long sticks, about 7 inches in length and about 1 inch thick. Wrap a slice of "bacon" around each dough stick. Roll each dough stick in parmesan cheese until well coated. If your dough isn't sticky enough and the parmesan needs some help sticking to the dough, brush with a very small amount of water, and then roll in parmesan cheese.

Arrange sticks evenly on a baking sheet lined with high temperature resistant parchment paper and bake for 8–10 minutes or until dough is cooked thoroughly and twists are golden brown. Whisk together mayonnaise, mustard and maple syrup to make dipping sauce. Serve twists with dipping sauce.

My Famous
Onion Dip and Spread

Serves 6–8

I serve this alongside hummus at almost every party or occasion that I host. Guess which one is always gone in minutes? I'll give you a hint—it's not the hummus. This onion dip is so versatile that it goes great with anything from crackers and chips to fresh vegetables. This dip can also be used as a spread—think sandwich spread or smeared on pieces of bread.

1 (8-ounce) container vegan cream cheese
1 small onion, finely chopped

¼ cup vegan bacon bits
1 tablespoon dried parsley

In a mixing bowl, combine cream cheese, onion and bacon bits. Transfer to serving bowl and top with parsley. Cover and refrigerate until ready to serve.

Breaded Mozzarella Sticks

Makes 10 mozzarella sticks

Oh yes, you read that right! Use your favorite vegan mozzarella cheese blocks and tomato marinara sauce and you have the appetizer that we have all been waiting for me to veganize for years—me included!

2 (10-ounce) blocks vegan mozzarella cheese	⅓ cup plain vegan milk
Olive oil cooking spray	2 cups Italian seasoned bread crumbs
2 tablespoons chia seeds	1 cup tomato marinara sauce

Cut each mozzarella cheese block into five sticks each, for a total of 10 sticks. Freeze until ready to use, for best result. Preheat oven to 400°F. Line a baking sheet with high temperature resistant parchment paper and spray generously with olive oil cooking spray.

Place chia seeds in blender or food processor and grind into a powder. In a small mixing bowl, combine chia seed powder and vegan milk; let sit until it reaches a gel or beaten "egg" consistency. Take each frozen mozzarella stick and dip it in chia "egg" and coat lightly, removing any excess, before rolling in bread crumbs and placing on oiled baking sheet. Once you have breaded all 10 sticks, bake for 3–5 minutes, then turn sticks and bake the other side for 3–5 minutes or until breading is golden and crispy, but before sticks get too melty. Serve with warmed tomato marinara sauce.

Crescent Roll Cinnamon
Buns with Caramel Drizzle,
page 69

Breakfast, Lunch and Brunch

What I love about the recipes in this next section is the way you can interchange them, swapping them in for whatever meal you fancy at the moment. Whether you're sleeping in on a Sunday or running late on a Monday, you can pick any of these recipes, according to your mood, and be good to go!

Fast Food Style
Breakfast Burritos
Makes 5 burritos

Breakfast burritos are my morning weakness. When I first became vegan, I thought that I would never be able to have them again—yet these taste so similar to the ones that I would grab at takeout restaurants that I almost take them for granted! (I know, I'm so spoiled.) Keep in mind, these burritos can be customized as well; this is just a basic breakfast burrito, so if you prefer some chopped bell pepper or even some jalapeno to make them spicy, feel free to go wild! I dig this recipe a lot; to me, it really tastes like the fast-food style breakfast meal that I remember…just way healthier with zero cholesterol!

3 tablespoons vegan butter
1 (15-ounce) block firm tofu, drained and crumbled
¼ teaspoon turmeric powder
½ teaspoon onion powder
¼ teaspoon garlic powder
1 tablespoon nutritional yeast

2 large vegan sausages, finely chopped
1 cup vegan cheddar cheese, shredded
5 medium-sized flour tortillas, warmed
Picante sauce (optional)
Salt and pepper, to taste

In a large skillet on medium heat, sauté tofu in butter and add turmeric, onion powder, garlic powder, nutritional yeast; season with salt and pepper. Add sausage to tofu mixture until slightly browned. Add cheese on top and cover to allow cheese to melt. Transfer tofu mixture to warmed tortillas and carefully fold them into burritos. Serve with picante sauce if desired.

Coffeehouse Style Pumpkin Cream Cheese Muffins

Makes 1 dozen muffins

This recipe was inspired by a muffin I saw in the bakery case at a coffee shop, which a friend of mine would often get with her coffee. I veganized the muffin based on the flavors that she described; having been a former pastry chef and owning my own vegan bakery really comes in handy! When I asked my friend to try my vegan version, she could not believe how much my recipe tasted like the one she would buy at the coffeehouse.

1 (8-ounce) container vegan cream cheese
½ cup powdered sugar
1 teaspoon vanilla extract
1 cup sugar
⅓ cup vegetable oil
1 cup pumpkin puree
¼ cup ground flaxseed mixed with ⅛

cup water
¼ cup soy milk
2 cups all-purpose flour
1 teaspoon baking soda
1 teaspoon pumpkin pie spice
¼ teaspoon salt
¼ cup pepitas (shelled, raw pumpkin seeds)

Preheat oven to 350°F and line a muffin pan with 12 cupcake/muffin liners or standard-sized baking cups.

In a small mixing bowl, combine cream cheese, powdered sugar and vanilla extract and set aside. In a large mixing bowl, combine vegetable oil, pumpkin puree, flaxseed and water mixture and soy milk. Combine flour, baking soda, pumpkin pie spice, and salt; add combined dry ingredients to the moist mixture, to make batter. Fill muffin cups evenly with batter. With the backside of a spoon, make a small well in the center of each muffin batter. Dollop cream cheese filling in the center wells of the muffin batters. Sprinkle pepitas around the top of the muffin, on the batter portion around the filling. Bake for about 15–20 minutes or until a cake tester comes out clean when poked into the bread part of muffin (not the filled centers).

Creamy Hot Cocoa
with the Works

Makes 4 drinks

I remember drinking these when I was a wee little tot. My mom would always send my brother and me outside on snowy days—with approximately a million layers of clothes on—and after plenty of snowball fights, sledding and snow angels, we would come inside to hot cocoa. And this wasn't the pre-made mixed cocoa, either; my mom made the good stuff! I created this recipe with those wonderful childhood memories in mind.

1 cup vegan semi-sweet chocolate chips
4 cups vanilla soy milk
¼ teaspoon vanilla extract
2 tablespoons sugar (optional or to taste)

⅛ teaspoon salt
8 large vegan marshmallows OR 16 mini vegan marshmallows
1 cup vegan whipped topping

In a large saucepan on low heat, combine all ingredients and whisk constantly until bubbly. Once bubbling, reduce heat even more, and continue to whisk constantly on simmer until chocolate chips and sugar (if using) are melted and well incorporated. Remove from heat and carefully pour into mugs using a spouted ladle. Top with marshmallows and whipped topping, divided evenly amongst four mugs.

S'mores Pancakes

Makes approximately 6 medium-sized pancakes

These campsite treats, with their gooey marshmallow, sweet chocolate and crunchy graham crackers have been all the rage for, like…forever. But let's face it—we don't all have the time to get a campfire started just because we want s'mores for breakfast. So what do we do? I'll tell ya—we fold those flavors into pancakes and eat s'mores whenever we want to!

¾ cup all-purpose flour
¼ cup vegan graham crackers, ground into fine crumbs
1 tablespoon sugar
2 tablespoons baking powder

⅛ teaspoon salt
1 cup vegan milk
2 tablespoons extra-virgin olive oil
¼ cup vegan mini marshmallows
¼ cup vegan mini chocolate chips

Preheat a well-greased frying pan, skillet or griddle to medium-high heat.

In a mixing bowl, combine flour, graham cracker crumbs, sugar, baking powder and salt. Combine milk and olive oil and add to dry mixture. Fold in marshmallows and chocolate chips.

Scoop about ¼ cup of batter and pour onto heated pan or griddle. Let that one side of pancake cook until you see bubbles start to form on top, then flip. The marshmallow and chocolate chips will be melty; the key is to be sure the pancake part is cooked thoroughly. Pancakes will cook about 3 minutes per side, but it can be more or less depending on your cooking device. Let the first pancake be your "tester" so you can judge the cook time for the rest of the batch. These pancakes are best served "as-is", since they *are* brimming with flavor, but you can serve them with butter, syrup or whipped topping, if desired.

The Perfect Vegan Pancake

Makes approximately 6 medium-sized pancakes

This recipe really does make the most fluffy and wonderful pancakes you've ever eaten. I played around with this recipe for a long time before finally achieving perfection, and I have been using it for years without fail. This recipe provides you with a base to make and serve with your favorite toppings like vegan butter and syrup or fruits and whipped topping. You can also fold mix-ins like chocolate chips or blueberries into the batter; I found that this recipe works splendidly for that! These are easy pancakes, too, so feel free to have them any morning, even on the weekdays!

1 cup all-purpose flour	⅛ teaspoon salt
1 tablespoon sugar	1 cup vegan milk
2 tablespoons baking powder	2 tablespoons extra-virgin olive oil

Preheat a lightly greased frying pan, skillet or griddle to medium-high heat. In a mixing bowl, combine flour, sugar, baking powder and salt. Combine milk and olive oil and add to dry mixture.

Scoop about ¼ cup of batter and pour onto heated pan or griddle. Let that one side of pancake cook until you see bubbles start to form on top, then flip. Pancakes will cook about 3 minutes per side, but it can be more or less depending on your cooking device. Let the first pancake be your "tester" so you can judge the cook time for the rest of the batch. Serve with your favorite pancake toppings, if desired.

Pumpkin Waffles

Makes approximately 6 waffles

These are waffles you can enjoy all year round (if you opt for canned pumpkin puree), and the recipe works with fresh pumpkin puree as well as other similar purees. I've used sweet potato in place of the pumpkin in this recipe and it tastes amazing; I love a recipe that you can play around with!

Dry ingredients
1 ½ cups all-purpose flour
¼ teaspoon baking soda
2 teaspoons baking powder
⅛ teaspoon salt
¼ teaspoon cinnamon
¼ teaspoon nutmeg
¼ cup brown sugar

Wet ingredients
2 tablespoons ground flaxseed, mixed
    with 1 tablespoon water (to be used
    as egg replacer)
3 tablespoons vegan butter, melted
3 tablespoons coconut oil, melted
1 ⅓ cup soymilk (or other vegan milk)
1 cup pumpkin puree (canned or
    fresh)
1 teaspoon vanilla extract

Follow your waffle maker manufacturer's instructions to preheat and use your waffle maker.

Mix dry ingredients together in one bowl and wet ingredients in another, separate bowl, before combining both wet and dry ingredients together. Use this batter in your waffle maker, following the manufacturer's instructions for cooking times. Cooking times will vary, but it is typically 2–4 minutes per waffle to cook them to perfection. Serve with your favorite waffle toppings.

Olive Oil Biscuits

Makes 10 biscuits

I perfected this biscuit recipe years ago, and it has been my go-to ever since. I wanted a biscuit that was flaky, a little fluffy and hearty; one that is versatile enough to be used at breakfast, while still providing a filling option for lunches or dinners as well. My personal favorite is slicing a biscuit in half and spreading it with either butter and jam or cream cheese and fruit spread.

2 cups all-purpose flour	½ cup extra-virgin olive oil
1 tablespoon baking powder	½ cup almond, soy or other vegan
½ teaspoon salt	milk

Preheat oven to 450°F. In a large mixing bowl, combine flour, baking powder and salt. Combine olive oil with milk and slowly add to flour mixture. With clean hands, mix thoroughly and gently knead dough.

On a lightly floured surface, roll out dough evenly, approximately ½ inch in thickness. Using a biscuit cutter or round cookie cutter, cut out 10 biscuit rounds. Place dough rounds on an ungreased baking sheet and arrange them about 1 inch apart. Bake for 10 minutes or until biscuits are lightly brown, have risen, and appear fluffy.

Crescent Roll Cinnamon Buns
with Caramel Drizzle

Makes 8 servings

The taste of these buns might make you think they're complicated and gourmet-prepared, but they're as effortless to make as they are impressive! When I created this recipe, I wanted to take the classic cinnamon bun and kick it up a notch; that's where the caramel drizzle comes in. It's almost too easy to devour several of these delectable breakfast treats without even realizing it—they are just that tasty!

1 (8-count) can crescent rolls	1 tablespoon coconut oil, melted
3 tablespoons vegan butter	1 tablespoon maple syrup
3 tablespoons sugar	1 tablespoon smooth almond butter
1 tablespoon brown sugar	¼ teaspoon vanilla extract
1 teaspoon cinnamon	2 tablespoons pecans, chopped
Pinch of nutmeg	(optional)

Preheat oven to 375°F. Line a baking sheet with high temperature resistant parchment paper. In a small mixing bowl, combine butter, sugar, brown sugar, cinnamon and nutmeg. Unroll each crescent dough triangle and spread sugar mixture evenly on one side; roll up into crescent shape and place each one on baking sheet, spaced at least 1 inch apart. Bake for 10–12 minutes or until dough is thoroughly cooked and outside of crescent cinnamon buns are golden brown.

   Melt coconut oil and whisk with maple syrup and vanilla extract; drizzle on top of crescent cinnamon buns and sprinkle with chopped pecans (if using).

Berry Lemon Crumble Loaf

Serves 6-8

Whenever I have overnight guests, be it during the holidays or just for a visit, I like to make a special breakfast for my guests to wake up to. I try to change it up—sometimes it's pancakes, sometimes waffles, other times muffins—but sometimes I will try to create something interesting on the fly. This berry lemon crumble loaf was one of those spontaneous moments of culinary concocting, and I am so happy with the way it turned out! My advice with this recipe is to ensure that the loaf is cooked thoroughly and is not gooey in the middle, which can happen when baking a bread loaf (especially when you have moist ingredients like yogurt and berries). During cooking, carefully check the middle of the loaf with a cake tester or a knife, and bake for longer if necessary.

2 cups all-purpose flour	**Topping**
½ cup sugar	¼ cup all-purpose flour
2 teaspoons baking powder	¼ cup sugar
½ teaspoon baking soda	2 tablespoons vegan butter
½ teaspoon salt	
½ cup vegan strawberry yogurt	
½ cup vegan blueberry yogurt	
¼ cup ground flaxseed	
½ cup vegetable oil	
Zest of 1 small lemon	
1 cup raspberries, fresh or frozen	

Preheat oven to 400°F. Line a 9 x 5-inch rectangular loaf pan with high temperature resistant parchment paper. In a large mixing bowl, combine 2 cups of flour, ½ cup of sugar, baking powder, baking soda and salt.

In a separate mixing bowl, combine yogurts with flaxseed then mix in oil and lemon zest. Add wet ingredients to dry ingredients in the large mixing bowl and stir until combined; fold in raspberries. Spread batter evenly in loaf pan.

In a small bowl, mix together ¼ cup of flour and ¼ cup of sugar, then cut in butter with a knife or fork until crumbly to make the topping. Sprinkle topping evenly on top of loaf. Bake for 50–60 minutes or until top is golden, center is thoroughly cooked, and a cake tester comes out clean when inserted in the middle of the loaf. Let loaf set for about 5 minutes before removing from pan. Slice and serve "as-is" or spread with a pat of vegan butter.

Eggless Salad
Serves 4

This recipe is my vegan take on the classic "egg" salad you might eat over a bed of lettuce or between bread as "egg" salad sandwiches. As a special note: you will notice the ingredient "black salt powder" featured in this recipe. Black salt is a type of rock salt that has almost exactly the same sulfurous taste that eggs do. A lot of black salt powders are produced in India, so if you have trouble finding this product in your local supermarket or health food store, you will surely find this sulfur-smelling salt at an Indian market or Middle Eastern food market. And remember, a little black salt powder goes a real long way, since it tends to be a little more salty than sea salt, so less is more!

1 (15-ounce) block firm tofu, drained
1 small onion, minced
¼ cup vegan mayonnaise
2 teaspoons Dijon mustard
¼ teaspoon turmeric powder
Black pepper, to taste
Black salt powder, to taste
Pinch of paprika, for garnish

In a mixing bowl, crumble tofu with a fork. When tofu is crumbly, mix in remaining ingredients (except for paprika). Serve over a bed of fresh greens and sprinkle a pinch of paprika on top as a garnish. You can also serve between bread to make eggless salad sandwiches.

Crunchy Chickenless Salad

Serves 4–6

When I came up with this recipe, what I had in mind was the classic "chicken" salad you might have over salad greens or on bread as a "chicken" salad sandwich. But I wanted to add some more crunch to it, something with more bite than celery and onion alone could provide. The addition of chopped apple to this salad definitely adds something special to this meal.

2 cups vegan chicken, cooked and cubed	¼ onion, finely chopped
½ cup celery, diced	½ cup vegan mayonnaise
1 small crisp apple, chopped	Salt and pepper, to taste

In a large mixing bowl, toss all ingredients together. Serve over a bed of lettuce or on toasted bread to enjoy as "chicken" salad sandwiches.

Tunaless Salad

Makes 4 servings

If you want to give this salad a more "fishy" and tuna-like flavor, you can add some nori or other seaweed flakes; however, the canned chickpeas really do make this tunaless salad taste very similar to tuna fish, except none of our fishy friends had to suffer for this delicious salad.

1 (15-ounce) can chickpeas, drained
1 stalk celery, finely chopped
1 small onion, finely chopped
½ cup vegan mayonnaise
1 teaspoon fresh lemon juice
¼ teaspoon garlic powder
Salt and pepper, to taste

In a mixing bowl, mash chickpeas with a fork until they look "flaky" in appearance, then add the remaining ingredients. Serve over a bed of fresh salad green or on sandwich bread to make tunaless salad sandwiches.

Sausage, Onions and Italian Sweet Peppers Sandwiches

Serves 4

Growing up as an Italian American, there were always Italian sweet peppers at our table, being served in various ways. These peppers resemble a large chili pepper but are light green in color, sweet in flavor and have nearly no heat. These peppers taste best when roasted or sautéed with olive oil, so this recipe really showcases these sweet peppers in all of their classic Italian glory. If you can't find these in your supermarket, don't stress out: you can substitute green bell peppers in this recipe. In fact, green peppers are commonly used in the non-vegan version of this dish at every Italian festival I have ever been to!

2 tablespoons extra-virgin olive oil	4 vegan sausage links, chopped
1 small onion, thinly sliced	4 large sandwich rolls OR 1 large loaf
1 garlic clove, minced	Italian bread
4 large green Italian sweet peppers, julienned	Vegan mayonnaise (optional)
	Salt and pepper, to taste

In a large frying pan on medium heat, sauté onion and garlic in olive oil until fragrant. Sauté peppers with onion and garlic until peppers are tender; add sausage and cook until sausage is browned. Season with salt and pepper to taste and serve on buns that or bread with mayonnaise spread on it, if you desire.

Citrus Glazed Tofu Fillets

Makes 4 tofu fillets

One day after returning home from the gym (yes, I do workout sometimes!) I wanted to make something delicious and high in protein to go with a vegetable side dish and a grain. I had a block of tofu on hand (what vegan doesn't?) and I wanted to make something easy but which also looks a little fancy and tastes really interesting. Hence, this recipe was born. This is great with a couple of sides or even over a bed of lettuce if you want to keep it light.

1 (15-ounce) block firm tofu, drained	1 teaspoon Dijon mustard
2 tablespoons orange marmalade	Salt and pepper, to taste

Cut tofu in half, then in half again lengthwise to make for rectangular tofu fillets of the same size. Combine marmalade, vinegar and mustard; brush this glaze all over tofu fillets. Season tofu with salt and pepper to taste. Broil on high for approximately 5 minutes on each side, or until tofu fillets are cooked to your liking.

Marinated Tomatoes and Mozzarella Salad

Serves 4

I have fond memories of my father making this salad when I was a child. He would pick the sweetest and most ripe tomatoes from our giant vegetable garden and we would make this salad together, usually at lunchtime. I am so happy to have veganized this salad in such a way that it tastes exactly like my childhood memories, and to now be able to share it with you.

8 plum tomatoes, quartered
¼ cup extra-virgin olive oil
2 tablespoons balsamic vinegar
2 tablespoons sugar
1 teaspoon dried basil OR 2
   tablespoons fresh basil, chopped

½ teaspoon onion powder
¼ teaspoon garlic powder
1 cup vegan mozzarella cheese,
   cubed
Salt and pepper, to taste

Toss all ingredients together in a large mixing bowl or serving dish (preferably glass) and refrigerate for at least 1 hour before serving.

Avocado, Kale and Tofu Salad

Serves 4

There's just something about avocado and kale together that I absolutely cannot resist. This salad is lovely and uncomplicated, but anything but ordinary. I find myself craving this salad on a regular basis, and that really says a lot about this recipe if it has a girl like me craving *anything* salad.

1 (10-ounce) bag kale greens, washed and torn into smaller pieces
2 ripe avocados, peeled and pitted
1 small onion, finely chopped
1 small red bell pepper, chopped

1 (15-ounce) block firm tofu, drained and cubed
2 tablespoons olive oil
Salt and pepper, to taste

Place kale on the bottom of a large salad bowl. In a separate mixing bowl, mash avocado and mix with chopped onion and pepper. Toss avocado mixture with kale until kale is coated well. In a large frying pan, sauté tofu in olive oil on medium heat, stirring frequently, until tofu is golden brown on all sides and slightly crisp. Top kale with tofu, and season with salt and pepper to taste.

Artisan BLT Sandwiches

Makes 4 sandwiches

The acronym "BLT" stands for Bacon, Lettuce and Tomato. This widely-known sandwich has stayed pretty popular since its birth in the early 1900s, when it evolved from a club sandwich. And making a BLT vegan is a cinch! After I started to get bored with the average BLT sandwich, I added some special touches to make it more like a gourmet dish. This is the type of BLT you would expect to see on the menu at a swanky restaurant in the city, but you can make it yourself in the comfort of your own home!

1 large loaf vegan ciabatta or artisan bread, sliced into 8 even slices	Olive oil cooking spray
¼ cup extra-virgin olive oil	8 strips vegan bacon
½ cup vegan mayonnaise	4 large romaine lettuce leaves
3 tablespoon fresh basil, sliced into thin strips	4 green olives, pitted, for garnish (optional)
1 large beefsteak or greenhouse tomato, cut into 4 even slices	

Preheat oven to 400°F and arrange bread slices in an ungreased baking sheet. Brush bread with olive oil and toast in oven for 5 minutes or until toasted.

Spray a medium frying pan with cooking spray and cook bacon slices until crisp, about 3 minutes per side; set aside. Spread mayonnaise on each toasted bread slice, sprinkle fresh basil on mayonnaise and top 4 bread slices with a slice of tomato. Add 2 slices of bacon and 1 leaf of romaine lettuce to the 4 bread slices with tomato on them; top them with remaining 4 bread slices (the ones with just mayonnaise and basil on them). If desired, top each sandwich with a green olive and secure with a toothpick, for garnish. (Do not eat the toothpick; just discard it!)

Chunky New England "Clam" Chowder

Serves 4-6

Growing up in New England, clam chowder was *the* soup whenever you went out to eat at a restaurant. Even small beach cafes and ice cream stands served it! When I started to miss the creaminess and chunks of potatoes this comforting soup provides, I knew I had to veganize it. I'm pretty sure this recipe is as close as one can get without putting any of our undersea friends in it. I sometimes serve this in sourdough bread bowls, which makes an already striking soup as filling as it is satisfying.

½ cup vegan butter
1 medium onion, chopped
2 garlic cloves, minced
1 (3.5-ounce) package oyster
   mushrooms, washed, destemmed
   and chopped
2 medium potatoes, peeled and cubed

1 sheet sushi nori, crumbled into small
   pieces
⅛ cup all-purpose flour
3 cups plain soy milk
1 cup vegetable broth
Salt and pepper, to taste

In a large saucepan on medium heat, melt butter and sauté onion and garlic until fragrant. Add mushrooms and potato to pan and sauté for 5 minutes, stirring frequently. Add nori and flour to pan and stir until thoroughly incorporated, then deglaze pan with milk and broth. Bring chowder to a boil, then reduce heat to low and simmer for 15–20 minutes or until potatoes are tender. Season with salt and pepper to taste.

Loaded Black Bean Soup

Serves 4

Any opportunity where you can add fun toppings to food stuff is one you should take! Life is too short not to indulge and add all your favorite toppings to your food. This soup tastes excellent, but with the addition of these toppings, it becomes over-the-moon delightful.

2 tablespoons extra-virgin olive oil
1 large onion, chopped
1 garlic clove, minced
2 (15-ounce) cans black beans, undrained
1 large tomato, chopped
½ teaspoon ground cumin
Salt and pepper, to taste

Toppings
4 teaspoons fresh cilantro, chopped
4 tablespoons vegan cheddar cheese, shredded
4 tablespoons salsa
4 tablespoons vegan sour cream
24 tortilla chips, crushed

In a large saucepan or small to medium-sized stockpot, sauté onions and garlic in olive oil on low heat until fragrant. Pour all contents of canned black beans (including liquid; do not drain) into saucepan or pot. Add tomato, cumin, salt and pepper to taste; bring to a gentle boil. Simmer on low-medium heat for 25 minutes, stirring occasionally. Serve in four large soup bowls and divide toppings atop of soup in each bowl.

Pasta Salad a la Peas

Serves 4-6

Pasta salad is the perfect salad for a lunch when you are craving a bit more, but still want to eat light. It's also a great choice for when you are in the mood for pasta, but don't care to prepare a heavier pasta dinner.

½ pound dry pasta (shells or elbows are ideal)
1 cup frozen peas, cooked and cooled
¼ cup onions, chopped
¼ cup vegan parmesan cheese, grated

1 cup vegan mayonnaise
1 teaspoon Dijon mustard
¼ tsp chili powder
Salt and pepper, to taste

Boil pasta according to package directions or until pasta is al dente; drain and rinse with cool water.

In a large mixing bowl, combine cooled pasta, peas, onions, parmesan, mayonnaise, mustard, chili powder, salt and pepper to taste. Chill for at least 3–4 hours in refrigerator prior to serving.

"Steak" Tips and
Sweet Potatoes, page 92

Main Meals

These next dishes are your heavy hitters—recipes that can hold their own, and never fail to satisfy. If you are looking for a dish to be the centerpiece of your table, there is something to suit any occasion you can imagine in this section.

"Steak" Tips and Sweet Potatoes

Serves 4–6

Though I like making this meal all year round, where this dish really shines is on chilly days; the flavors just seem to warm the soul. I put this recipe together one day when I had an abundance of sweet potatoes in my pantry and wanted to find a different way of using them in a savory meal. This recipe is a breeze to prepare but bursting with flavor. If you want to really kick it up a notch, serve with fresh bread buttered with maple butter. (Maple butter is easy to make; you just take vegan butter and a little maple syrup and whip it together; it is outrageous how well this simple-made butter, smeared on bread, mingles with this dish.)

2 tablespoons olive oil	¾ cup vegetable broth
3 cups beefless product, cubed	¼ teaspoon cinnamon
1 large onion, thinly sliced	1 tablespoon corn starch
2 large sweet potatoes, peeled and cubed	2 tablespoons water
	Salt and pepper, to taste

In a large pot, brown onion and beefless product in olive oil on medium heat for 5 minutes, stirring occasionally. Add sweet potatoes, broth and cinnamon to pot and cook until sweet potatoes are tender, stirring occasionally.

In a small bowl, wish together corn starch and water then add to pot; combine well. Simmer on low until thickened. Season with salt and pepper to taste. Can be served "as-is", with crusty bread or over a bed of rice.

Harvest Apple and Acorn Squash Soup

Makes 4–6 servings

This soup tastes like it came straight from the orchard store café! When you can get fresh, local acorn squash in season, you might notice a superior taste; however, this is not necessary, and having made this soup many times both ways, I can say that it always comes out divine.

3 tablespoons vegan butter
2 tablespoons garlic, diced
1 large onion, diced
1 acorn squash, peeled and chopped
4 apples (I recommend a combination of golden delicious and gala), peeled, cored and chopped

3 cups vegetable stock
1½ cups water
¼ teaspoon ground ginger
¼ teaspoon ground cinnamon
¼ teaspoon ground cumin
⅛ teaspoon ground nutmeg
Salt and pepper, to taste

In a large stockpot on medium heat, sauté garlic, onion, squash and apples in butter for 5 minutes, stirring frequently. Add the remaining ingredients and bring to a gentle boil. Reduce heat and simmer for 20 minutes or until squash is tender. Carefully, with a handheld immersion blender or in a food processor in batches, blend soup until smooth. Return to pot and heat on low heat for a few minutes until thoroughly warmed.

Italian Rustic Easter "Ham" Pie (Pizzagaina)

Serves 12–14

Pizzagaina is something my Italian family made every year around Easter. Traditionally, this ham pie is made with meat, cheese and eggs, and is chock full of cholesterol and animal products. People did not believe me when I told them that I'd veganized this classic recipe, especially my family. Everyone thought it was impossible to take a ham pie and turn it vegan. I am proud to say that I've managed to not only do just that, but also make it taste amazing *and* practically indistinguishable from the original. Of all the recipes in this book, this one may be the best proof that there is no need whatsoever to eat animal products. Everything can be made vegan; nothing is impossible.

4 cups all-purpose flour
½ cup vegan butter
1 cup warm water
1 (15-ounce) block firm tofu, drained
1 large vegan sausage link, diced
1 (5.5-ounce) package vegan deli ham slices, diced
1 (5.5-ounce) package vegan deli bologna slices, diced

1 cup vegan mozzarella cheese, shredded
¼ cup vegan cheddar cheese, cubed
¼ vegan Monterey jack cheese, cubed
¼ cup vegan Havarti cheese, cubed
1 tablespoon extra-virgin olive oil
Black pepper, to taste

Preheat oven to 400°F. Lightly grease a 9 x 13-inch baking dish. In a large mixing bowl, combine flour, butter and warm water to make crust dough; knead with clean hands, divide into two balls of equal size and let rest.

Take one of the dough balls and spread dough evenly in the bottom and up the sides of baking dish. In a food processor, blend tofu until smooth and pour into a large mixing bowl. Add remaining ingredients (except for olive oil) to tofu and mix well. Pour tofu, "meat" and cheese mixture atop crust dough in baking dish and spread evenly. Roll out remaining dough ball to the shape and size of the baking dish, and place on top of the pie. Brush the top of the pie with olive oil and bake covered for 20 minutes.

Reduce oven heat to 350°F and bake for 45 more minutes, uncovered for the last 15 minutes. Let pie cool and set for about 1–2 hours before cutting into squares. Traditionally this pie is served cold, after being refrigerated, however is delicious when enjoyed warm as well.

One Pot "Steak" and Potatoes with Mushrooms

Makes 4–6 servings

We all know that one person. The steak and potato individual who proclaims that they "could never go vegan" because they despise vegetables and say they only really eat steak and potatoes. Go ahead; fool them with this recipe. (And remind them that the potato is a vegetable, while you're at it!)

3 garlic cloves, chopped	1 cup mushrooms (like white button or baby Portobello), washed and quartered
1 large onion, chopped	
3 tablespoons extra-virgin olive oil	
2 large all-purpose potatoes, washed and cubed	½ tablespoon vegan Worcestershire sauce
2 cups beefless product, cubed or in chunks	¾ cup vegetable broth
	Salt and pepper, to taste

In a large pot, sauté garlic and onion in olive oil on medium heat until fragrant, then add potatoes. Season with salt and pepper to taste and cook for 20 minutes or until potatoes are tender, stirring frequently. Add beefless product, mushrooms and Worcestershire sauce; cover and cook until beefless mushrooms are tender and beefless is cooked well and is browned. Deglaze pan with broth halfway through cooking. Serve with ketchup or sriracha sauce and with a nice piece of soft buttered bread.

Peanut Butter Tofu Stir-fry

Makes 4 servings

This is a weird recipe, but it is so delicious! My husband and I have been making this for many years, ever since we first became vegan. Back in the day, tofu was thought of as being a little lame. Being plant-based wasn't always as cool as it is now, and the availability of vegan food made things much harder to come by. The "it" protein was tofu, no question, but you had to really jazz it up and think very creatively in order to avoid becoming mundane. My husband and I were creating different tofu recipes, and this is one of his creations. I am so grateful that he invented this stir-fry recipe because it is far from boring. Just try to disregard the more unusual ingredients while you're making it, and you will be pleasantly surprised with the end result.

1 (15-ounce) block firm tofu, drained
¼ cup extra-virgin olive oil
½ cup creamy peanut butter
3 tablespoons soy sauce
2 tablespoons ketchup
2 teaspoons Dijon mustard
1 teaspoon onion powder
½ teaspoon garlic powder
2 cups stir-fry vegetables, fresh or frozen
2 tablespoons vegetable oil
Black pepper, to taste

In a large bowl, combine olive oil, peanut butter, soy sauce, ketchup, mustard, onion powder, garlic powder and black pepper; add tofu and gently toss until covered in marinade. Place in refrigerator to marinate for 4 hours for best results; if short on time, marinate chilled while you cook the vegetables.

In a wok on medium heat, sauté vegetables in vegetable oil, stir-frying until tender. Add tofu and all marinade sauce to wok with vegetables. Stir-fry until combined and tofu is hot and well-cooked. Serve over rice.

Gingery Fishless and Mushrooms

Makes 4–6 servings

This dish is just insanely delicious. The recipe is simplistic yet bursting with flavor. I also find that it is a nice way to prepare vegan fishless products. Let's face it; there's only so much you can tolerate eating that fake fish with lemon or homemade vegan tartar sauce. You have to change it up sometimes; real talk.

½ cup vegan butter
1 small onion, chopped
2 cups fresh mushrooms, washed and sliced
2 (8-ounce) cans sliced bamboo shoots, drained

2 cups fishless product, chopped
1 tablespoon fresh ginger, minced
1 tablespoon corn starch
½ cup vegetable stock
Salt and pepper, to taste

In a large frying pan, pot or wok on medium heat, melt butter and sauté onion until fragrant; add mushrooms and cook until tender, stirring frequently. Add bamboo shoots, fishless product, soy sauce, and fresh ginger; stir-fry until well combined and cooked thoroughly.

Add cornstarch to vegetable stock and stir into pan. Reduce heat and simmer until sauce thickens. If needed or desired, season with salt and pepper to taste. Serve over rice.

"Chicken" Alfredo over Spaghetti Squash "Pasta"

Serves 2–4

I love, love, *love* doing this sort of thing! You take a heavy meal like "chicken" Alfredo, lighten it up a little bit by making wildly amazing "pasta" out of spaghetti squash, and you get to eat buttered bread or buttery breadsticks with your meal without feeling too guilty! It's genius, right?

1 medium or large spaghetti squash	1 ½ cups vegan mozzarella cheese, shredded
2 tablespoons extra-virgin olive oil	¼ teaspoon onion powder
¼ cup vegan butter	¼ teaspoon garlic powder
¼ cup vegan cream cheese	1 cup vegan chicken strips, cooked and chopped
⅓ cup plain vegan milk	Salt and pepper, to taste
¼ cup vegan parmesan cheese, grated	

Preheat oven to 450°F. Cut squash in half lengthwise; remove and discard seeds, drizzle with olive oil, season with salt and pepper to taste, and bake for 30–40 minutes or until tender but still slightly firm.

In a medium saucepan on low heat, melt butter. Add cream cheese to melted butter and whisk together. Slowly whisk in milk, parmesan, mozzarella, onion powder, garlic powder, salt and pepper. Cook, whisking frequently, until sauce is thick and bubbly, then add "chicken" and cook until warmed thoroughly, while stirring constantly. Remove from heat.

When squash is cool enough to handle safely, remove "spaghetti" strands by using a fork and dragging it into squash in long stroking movements. Once squash "spaghetti" strands are removed, put them into a large serving bowl and top with the "chicken" and Alfredo sauce mixture. Toss before serving.

Easy Artisan Sicilian Pizza

Serves 4-6

One time at a fancy Sicilian restaurant, I saw all these other dishes on the menu that incorporated delicious fresh pairings with the choices that unfortunately had animal products in them, but the vegan options were so boring. I went home and thought of the ingredients I saw on the menu, artichokes and capers, and curated a Sicilian inspired pizza without the animal products. Since many of these ingredients are easy to find in the Italian isle of any grocery store, this recipe is a cinch to make, however the flavor combination will have your taste buds doing a victory dance in your mouth! Vegans can too have gourmet pizza and we don't have to get all dressed up to go to the stylish restaurant to achieve it. Don't skip the 'seasoning with salt and pepper' step at the end of this recipe – it gives this pizza extra oomph.

20 ounces prepared pizza dough
½ cup vegan cream cheese
3 ounces tomato paste
2 teaspoon dried Italian seasoning
2 tablespoon extra-virgin olive oil
8.5 ounces artichoke hearts,
   quartered

6 ounces roasted red peppers
10 Kalamata olives, pitted & sliced
2 tablespoons capers, drained
4 ounces vegan mozzarella cheese,
   sliced or shredded
Salt and pepper, to taste

Preheat oven to 450°F. Roll out dough in a circular shape on a floured surface, to desired thickness. Place dough on a greased and floured pizza pan or on a pizza stone. Let dough rest for 3–5 minutes.

Mix cream cheese, tomato paste, Italian seasoning, and 1 tablespoon of olive oil in a small mixing bowl; spread evenly on dough. Top pizza with artichokes, red peppers, olives, capers and cheese. Drizzle with remaining olive oil. Season the top with salt and pepper. Bake for 10–15 minutes or until crust is golden and the cheese is bubbly and melted. Let pizza sit to settle for a few moments before slicing.

Split Pea Soup
with Tempeh "Bacon"

Serves 8

What an underrated soup split pea is. A mighty tasty soup indeed, but not only that, split peas contain 16 grams of protein and 16 grams of fiber per 1 cup cooked! Plus, the shelf life on a properly stored bag of dried split peas is pretty good, at 1 year (though some people say that when stored with oxygen absorption, the shelf-life is 10 years or longer!)

1 tablespoon olive oil	2 cups dried split peas
2 teaspoons vegan Worcestershire sauce	12 cups water
1 tablespoon maple syrup	1 large onion, finely chopped
1 tablespoon soy sauce	½ cup celery, finely chopped
1 (8-ounce) package tempeh, thinly sliced	1 teaspoon dried parsley
	Black pepper, to taste
	Salt and pepper, to taste

Preheat oven to 350°F. In a medium mixing bowl, combine olive oil, Worcestershire sauce, maple syrup, soy sauce and black pepper; toss tempeh slices in sauce mixture and coat well. Arrange tempeh evenly in a greased baking pan and drizzle with any remaining sauce. Bake for 20 minutes, turning once halfway through; "bacon" is done when crispy and browned.

In a large stockpot, bring split peas and water to a gentle boil, and continue to boil for 5 minutes. Add onion, celery and parsley to soup; cover and simmer for 1 hour or until split peas are tender and liquid is partially reduced. Serve with tempeh "bacon" crumbled on top.

Mom's Cheesy "Chicken" and Stuffing Casserole

Makes 8 servings

My mom made this for dinner throughout my childhood, and though I always loved the flavors, I wasn't a fan of the chicken part. It always freaked me out to find a vein or a red bloody part as I was eating, and even as a kid, I realized that I was not meant to eat animal products. Years later, having recreated this dish and countless others that I used to savor in my past, I can say for sure something that I've always known: it isn't the animal products that I craved; it was the preparation and the flavors in the sauces. In other words, it was the non-vegan products in the meal that made me like it. I really think that is the case for so many people out there. Making recipes vegan really can change the whole world for the better, because if someone can enjoy the same flavors they would normally, but in vegan-form, I think you'd see a lot less animals on people's plates.

---

8 vegan chicken "breasts" or fillets
8 slices vegan Swiss cheese
1 (4-ounce) can mushrooms (pieces & stems), drained
1 tablespoon vegan butter, melted
1 cup vegan cream
1 tablespoon all-purpose flour

1 cup vegetable stock
⅛ teaspoon dried thyme
⅛ teaspoon black pepper
½ (14-ounce) bag cubed and seasoned stuffing mix
Olive oil cooking spray

Preheat oven to 350°F and grease a 9 x 13-inch baking dish. Arrange "chicken" evenly in baking dish and top each piece with a slice of cheese. In a food processor or blender, puree mushrooms, butter, cream, flour, stock, thyme and black pepper; pour on top of "chicken" and toss with stuffing so bread cubes can absorb liquid. Rearrange in pan in an even layer. Spray casserole generously with olive oil cooking spray. Cover and bake for 30 minutes, baking uncovered for last 5 minutes, or until casserole is bubbly and topping is golden brown. Serve "as-is", over rice or with bread.

Maple Glazed
"Boneless Spareribs"

Makes 4 servings

Once you try this recipe, you are going to want to send me a thank you e-mail. So I'll save you the trouble and reply right here, right now: I know; and you are welcome.

½ cup soy sauce
2 tablespoons red wine
2 teaspoons garlic, minced
¼ cup maple syrup

2 pounds beefless product, strips or cubes
2 tablespoons extra-virgin olive oil

In a large mixing bowl, combine soy sauce, red wine, garlic and maple syrup to make a marinade. Add beefless product to marinade and cover; refrigerate for at least 1 hour.

In a large skillet on low heat, add olive oil and remove beefless product with a slotted spoon, adding to skillet; reserve marinating liquid. Stir-fry for 15 minutes, adding marinating liquid to pan as needed until beefless is browned. Serve over rice or noodles and with your favorite vegetable side dish.

Jenn Mann's Chickenless Cacciatore tossed with Angel Hair Spaghetti Pasta

Serves 4–6

I created this cacciatore recipe for my vegan friend, Dr. Jenn Mann. Dr. Jenn is famously busy—between being a mom, a psychotherapist to the stars, working with celebrity couples on shows like VH1's *Couple's Therapy*, making television or speaking appearances, hosting her radio show, being the author of several bestselling books, and the creator of popular app No More Diets, designing fashions for her eco-friendly clothing line, Retail Therapy, and being an animal rights activist—it's no surprise that she doesn't have time to be slaving away in the kitchen.

I wanted her to have a dish that's quick and easy to make with her family, but that tastes flavorful and gourmet. The chickenless is already sliced in strips, and since it uses simple ingredients, throwing this dish together is just as enjoyable as eating it.

You can follow Jenn on Twitter @DrJennMann, or check out her website, DoctorJenn.com.

1 pound dry angel hair spaghetti pasta	¼ cup vegetable stock
3 tablespoons extra-virgin olive oil	2 tablespoons fresh basil, chopped
2 garlic cloves, minced	1 tablespoon fresh parsley, chopped
1 large onion, finely chopped	2 tablespoons capers, drained and minced
1 pound chickenless strips	2 tablespoons vegan butter, melted
2 cups ripe tomatoes, diced	Salt and pepper, to taste

Boil water to cook pasta according to package directions until al dente. In a large saucepan on medium heat, saute garlic and onions until fragrant then add chickenless strips and tomatoes; cook until chickenless strips are lightly browned and tomatoes are tender. Deglaze pan with vegetable stock and reduce heat to low. Add basil, parsley, capers, salt and pepper to taste and warm thoroughly.

Remove saucepan from heat. Drain pasta and add to saucepan; pour on melted butter. Toss pasta, sauce and melted butter until combined well. Serve using a pasta fork.

Stuffed Cabbage Rolls

Makes 12 stuffed cabbage rolls

This is a great recipe to make when you have leftover rice that you're trying to use up before it spoils. Any time you have cooked rice that you don't want going to waste, go out and grab yourself a cabbage and the rest of the ingredients for this yummy main meal!

12 large cabbage leaves, removed from head and washed	2 cups "beef" crumbles
2 tablespoons olive oil	1 cup cooked rice, white or brown
1 small onion, chopped	3 cups tomato marinara sauce (any prepared or jar sauce will do fine)
1 garlic clove, chopped	Salt and pepper, to taste

Preheat oven to 350°F and grease a 9 x 13-inch baking dish. In a large pot, bring water (enough to cover cabbage leaves) to a boil and boil cabbage leaves until they are soft, approximately 10 minutes. Drain water and set leaves aside.

In a medium saucepan on medium heat, sauté onions and garlic in olive oil until tender. Add "beef" crumbles and sauté until browned. Remove from heat and mix in rice, salt and pepper. Allow to cool enough to handle safely. With clean hands, ball rice and "beef" mixture and stuff cabbage leaves, rolling and folding them into little "packages", similar to how you would fold a burrito. Place cabbage rolls in greased baking dish then pour marinara sauce over them. Cover and bake for 45 minutes to 1 hour.

Sausage YUMbo Gumbo
Makes 6 servings

There isn't anything in this gumbo *called* YUMbo, I was just trying to be funny. Get it? Because the gumbo is yummy, so it is…yum, yumbo gumbo. *awkward silence* *author whistles and walks away*

Seriously, though—this is an *amazing* gumbo. Feel free to add more spice if you like the heat and spiciness. You can also add file powder (ground leaves from the sassafras tree), but I have made it without file powder more times than not using this recipe, and it is such a hit with the eaters.

⅓ cup extra-virgin olive oil
⅓ cup all-purpose flour
2 large onions, chopped
2 garlic cloves, minced
1 large green bell pepper, chopped
1 (14-ounce) package vegan
   sausages, chopped
2 cups tomatoes, chopped

¾ cup celery, chopped
1 (16-ounce) bag frozen cut okra
2 quarts vegetable broth
½ teaspoon ground cayenne pepper
   (more or less depending on your
   spice preference)
1½ teaspoon dried Italian seasoning
Salt and pepper, to taste

In a large saucepan on medium heat, stir olive oil and flour together to make a roux. Keep stirring the oil and flour mixture until it begins to toast and turn a golden brown color, then add onions, garlic and bell pepper; roux will coat onions, garlic and pepper then cook until fragrant, stirring constantly.

Add chopped sausage, tomatoes, celery, okra, broth, cayenne pepper, Italian seasoning, salt and pepper to taste, to saucepan. Bring gumbo to a boil then reduce heat to low. Simmer for 20 minutes or until vegetables are tender. Serve with bread or with rice.

Curry Not-Chicken

Serves 4–6

I'm a huge curry fan. Curries that are on the sweeter side work really well in this recipe; however, if you prefer a spicier curry, curries with heat will work nicely, too. It's a really versatile curry "chicken" offering, one where the heat can be easily customized to suit your taste. I like making this recipe using different curries to experience the different flavors, so I find this to be a really fun recipe to play around with.

¼ cup vegan butter
1 large onion, chopped
1 large green bell pepper, chopped
2 cups vegan chicken strips
1 tablespoon all-purpose flour
½ tablespoon curry powder

1 teaspoon fine sea salt
¼ cup water
⅛ cup fresh lemon juice
1 cup tomato marinara sauce
1 garlic clove, minced

In a large saucepan on medium heat, melt butter and sauté onion and bell pepper until tender. Add "chicken" strips and stir-fry until it is lightly browned. Stir in flour, curry powder and salt then slowly stir in water; continue stirring until you reach a paste consistency. Add tomato sauce and garlic, reduce heat to low and bring to a simmer. Continue to simmer on low heat for 20 minutes, stirring occasionally. Serve over rice.

Gourmet "Beef" Stroganoff
Serves 4-6

This recipe is such a timeless classic that many believed it could not be veganized. Surprisingly, this was actually an easy recipe to make vegan! I've been making this "beef" stroganoff for so many years now and it really is a go-to meal in my household. What I like about this stroganoff is that it is hearty, filling and fulfilling. but so convenient to put together. Anytime that I make it for guests, they always comment about how amazing it tastes. You can see how people feel special when you make it for them, like this is some sort of gourmet meal. So you see, I really had no choice but to call it gourmet!

2 cups of beefless product, cubes or chunks	1 small onion, chopped
¼ cup vegan butter	1 cup vegetable stock
2 cups fresh mushrooms, washed and sliced	1 cup vegan sour cream
	2½ tablespoons all-purpose flour

In a large saucepan on medium heat, sauté beefless product in butter until lightly browned, then add mushrooms and onion; sauté until onion and mushrooms are tender. Blend in vegetable stock, sour cream and flour and continue to cook on medium heat until bubbly and sauce slightly thickens. Serve over pasta, noodles or rice.

Broccoli, Tofu and Coconut Slow Cooker Soup

Serves 4–6

Broccoli and tofu mingle with the other delightful ingredients in this recipe, like coconut milk and spices, to make for one amazing soup. This is a slow cooker soup, which makes it super easy to prepare. It doesn't get much better than this, folks!

½ onion, chopped
3 tablespoon extra-virgin olive oil
1 (16-ounce) bag frozen broccoli
1 (15-ounce) block firm tofu, drained & cubed
2 large Portobello mushroom caps, sliced
1 (13.5-ounce) can coconut milk
½ cup vegetable broth

1 tablespoon sweet curry powder
2 teaspoons dried Italian seasoning
1 tablespoon soy sauce
1 teaspoon garlic powder
½ teaspoon onion powder
½ teaspoon ground cumin
¼ teaspoon ground ginger
1 tablespoon maple syrup
Salt and pepper, to taste

Place all ingredients in slow cooker and gently stir to combine. Cook on high heat setting for 4 hours or low heat setting for 6–7 hours, or until vegetables are tender. This soup can be served by itself, with noodles or rice, or with buttered bread.

Classic Chili

Makes 4–6 servings

There's a few things you can do with this chili recipe to truly make it your own, including adjusting the spiciness to your taste by using more or less chili powder. As well as being served "as-is", this chili can alternatively be served loaded with your favorite toppings like crackers, crumbles of veggie bacon, shredded cheddar cheese or generous dollops of sour cream. You can also top with fresh garnishes like herbs such as cilantro, parsley, chives or dill.

2 tablespoons extra-virgin olive oil	2 tablespoons brown sugar
1 small onion, chopped	1 teaspoon ground cumin
1 garlic clove, minced	1 teaspoon chili powder
1 (12-ounce) package "beef" crumbles	1 teaspoon paprika
1 (28-ounce) can crushed tomatoes	1 teaspoon dried basil
1½ cups water	½ teaspoon dried oregano
1 (15-ounce) can kidney beans, drained and rinsed	Salt and pepper, to taste

In a large saucepan on medium heat, sauté onions and garlic in olive oil until fragrant. Add crumbles to pan and cook, stirring constantly, until slightly brown. Add remaining ingredients and simmer on low for about 25 minutes, or until flavors are well combined.

Dad's Tastes-Like-Sunday Sauce

Makes enough for 1 pound cooked pasta

I bet you are wondering at the reason behind the name "Tastes-Like-Sunday Sauce."
Growing up as an Italian-American, the entire family was all well aware of my grandmother's Sunday pasta sauce, including how long it took to make. It would simmer on
the stove from the wee hours of the morning until it was time to eat our pasta dinner,
and with that slow cooking process came immense, rich flavor. Well, my father invented
his version of Sunday sauce, except his recipe takes just minutes to make! It is quite
remarkable how my dad was able to develop the same lovely flavors of a long simmering
sauce in a quick pasta sauce; he credits his technique. I wanted to share my dad's secret
recipe with the world. To all of the Italian grandmas out there in the world, we give our
sincerest apologies.

1 (28-ounce) can crushed tomatoes	1 teaspoon garlic powder
3 tablespoons extra-virgin olive oil	1 teaspoon onion powder
2 tablespoons dried parsley	1/8 teaspoon dried oregano
1 tablespoon dried basil	1/8 teaspoon baking soda
1 tablespoon brown sugar	Salt and pepper, to taste

Dump all ingredients into a large saucepan; mix and bring to a boil, stirring
frequently. Boil for a few moments longer and then remove from heat. And it
is done!

Cheesy Summer Vegetable Bake

Serves 4-6

Dinners like this dish are best in the summer. Fast, easy, and you can conveniently grab most of these ingredients at the farmers market on your way home from enjoying a day outside. Of course, you can make this recipe all year long, not just in the summertime. Go ahead, I won't tell anyone if you do. (I do it, too!)

2 cups zucchini, chopped
1 cup sweet tomatoes, chopped
1 large bell pepper (any color), chopped
1 garlic clove, minced
2 tablespoons fresh parsley, chopped
2 tablespoons fresh basil, chopped

1 cup vegan mozzarella cheese, shredded
2 cups bread crumbs
2 tablespoons extra-virgin olive oil
Salt and pepper, to taste

Preheat oven to 350°F and grease a large casserole dish or a 9 x 13-inch baking dish. In a large mixing bowl, combine zucchini, tomatoes, bell pepper, garlic, parsley, basil, cheese, salt and pepper; pour into greased baking dish and spread mixture evenly. Top with bread crumbs and spread evenly over top of vegetable mixture; drizzle with olive oil. Cover and bake for 40 minutes, the last 10 minutes uncovered, or until vegetables are tender and bread crumb topping is golden brown.

Portuguese Kale Soup

Makes approximately 6 servings

This recipe is an example of how a recipe can seem so simple and ordinary but, once you taste it, you find it is just bursting with delicious and well-developed flavors. There's a few adaptations to keep in mind in case you have most of the ingredients for this soup, but have a different "this" or "that" on hand. For example, the recipe calls for potatoes and you can use white, red or sweet potatoes. For the beans in this recipe, I have used canned kidney, navy, cannellini, pinto and even chickpeas! Virtually any bean works great in this meal, so feel free to stick with the recipe, while using your favorite beans or what you have on hand at the time.

¼ cup extra-virgin olive oil
2 medium onions, chopped
4 garlic cloves, chopped
2 cups beefless product OR vegan sausage, cut into large chunks
4 large potatoes, washed and cubed
6 cups kale, washed and stems removed
1 (15-ounce) can kidney beans (or other flavor), drained and rinsed
4 cups vegetable broth
2 cups water
2 dried bay leaves
Salt and pepper, to taste

In a large stock pot, sauté onions and garlic in olive oil on low/medium heat, stirring frequently, for about 10 minutes. Add in beefless product and sauté until lightly browned. Add remaining ingredients and bring to a boil. Reduce heat to low and simmer soup for 20–30 minutes, or until potatoes are tender. Serve with crusty bread.

No Boil Lasagna

Makes 8 servings

I designed this recipe to be easy, so you can buy the less expensive lasagna noodles and not the pricey no-boil ones, enjoying the ease of putting together your lasagna casserole without boiling anything. It really doesn't get much easier than this recipe. I even designed the tofu "ricotta" mixture such that you can prepare it without a food processor without losing any of the taste or texture.

2 (24-ounce) jars tomato marinara
   sauce
½ cup water
1 teaspoon garlic powder
1 teaspoon dried Italian seasoning
1 (15-ounce) block firm tofu, drained
½ cup vegan cream cheese
3 cups vegan mozzarella cheese,
   shredded

1 teaspoon dried parsley
3 tablespoons extra-virgin olive oil
1 package uncooked lasagna noodles
1½ cups refrigerated vegan ground
   "beef" crumbles
Salt and pepper, to taste

Preheat oven to 350°F and grease a 9 x 13-inch baking dish. In a large saucepan, combine tomato marinara sauce, water, garlic powder and Italian seasoning and bring to a gentle boil; simmer for 10 minutes, stirring occasionally, then remove from heat.

In a large mixing bowl, mash tofu until finely crumbled and mix in cream cheese, 2 cups of mozzarella cheese, parsley, 2 tablespoons of olive oil, salt and pepper to taste, to make ricotta. Spread 1 cup of the marinara sauce evenly in the baking dish. Place 3 lasagna noodles on the sauce, lining them up beside each other and spaced out evenly. Cover with another scoop of marinara sauce. Spread about ⅓⅓ of the tofu ricotta mixture and sprinkle about a third of the "beef" grounds on top of that. Spread more tomato sauce on top, 3 more lasagna noodles, more ricotta mixture, more beef grounds, more sauce, then noodles again, repeating until ricotta and "beef" mixtures run out. The top layer of lasagna should have noodles and the remainder of marinara sauce (about 1 cup); top with 1 cup of shredded mozzarella cheese. Drizzle 1 tablespoon of olive oil over top of lasagna. Cover and bake for 50 minutes, then bake uncovered for an additional 15 minutes more. Let lasagna sit for 15 minutes to set and cool down a bit before cutting and serving.

Slow Cooker Two Cheese Broccoli and Cheddar Soup

Makes 6–8 servings

Stop me if you've heard this before: "I *would* go vegan…but I can't give up my dairy products." I was told something similar just recently; someone told me that they would like to go vegan, but can't find their favorite soup, broccoli and cheddar, in a vegan version. They also mentioned that making this soup is way too hard. So after hearing this, I just had to veganize this soup. Not only that, I wanted to make it a slow cooker recipe so that it is super easy and convenient to make. There should be no excuses keeping you from something that you really want to do. If going vegan is what this person wants to do, I'll happily recreate their favorite soup to help get them there! As a plus, now we all get to enjoy a super delicious, comforting, creamy and cheesy vegan soup that is such a breeze to make.

Olive oil cooking spray
¼ cup vegan butter
2 medium onions, chopped
2½ cups soy milk
3 cups vegetable broth
2 cups frozen or fresh broccoli, finely chopped
¼ teaspoon salt
¼ teaspoon black pepper
1 teaspoon garlic powder
2 cups vegan cheddar cheese, shredded
1 cup vegan mozzarella cheese, shredded

Grease slow cooker generously by spraying with cooking spray. In a large frying pan on medium heat, sauté onions in butter for 5 minutes, stirring occasionally. Stir in flour, stirring constantly, until it completely covers onions and begins to slightly brown. Slowly stir in 1½ cups of soy milk until mixture is thick, then carefully pour into slow cooker. Add vegetable broth, broccoli, salt, pepper and garlic powder to slow cooker and mix. Cook on high heat setting for 3–4 hours or until broccoli is tender; soup should be bubbly. Finally, add cheeses and stir until they are thoroughly melted. If needed, season with additional salt and pepper to taste.

If you'd like an even creamier and smoother soup, you can blend with an immersion blender or with a blender in batches, to all or some of the soup. I usually skip this and enjoy it as it is, especially if the broccoli was chopped finely and is cooked until very tender. If you use fresh broccoli instead of frozen, the soup tends to need more cooking in the slow cooker, so cooking time may vary depending on your choice of ingredients and the type of slow cooker you are using.

One Pot Taco Soup

Makes 4 servings

I absolutely love taco nights and I really appreciate the many flavors it offers, but sometimes making separate bowls for all of the toppings can be a hassle after a long workday. That's why, when I created this taco soup, I made it a one pot soup! This recipe takes very well to customization; you can add vegan sour cream, and any other toppings that you would like. What's presented here is an easy recipe that does a decent job at embracing the main flavors of tacos without making back-breaking work out of it.

---

2 vegan butter
1 pound vegan beef crumbles
1 (14-ounce) can vegan tomato soup
½ cup mild picante sauce, jar or freshly made
6 medium-sized flour tortillas, chopped
½ cup water

½ teaspoon onion powder
1 cup vegan cheddar cheese, shredded
¼ cup fresh cilantro, finely chopped (optional)
Salt and pepper, to taste

In a large saucepan, sauté "beef" in butter on medium heat until browned; stir in tomato soup, picante sauce, chopped tortillas, water, onion powder, salt and pepper to taste (if needed). Cook on medium heat and bring to a gentle boil, then simmer on low heat for 10 minutes, stirring frequently. Mix in cheddar cheese and serve in large soup bowls. Top with fresh cilantro, if using.

Easy Ratatouille Stew

Makes 6–8 servings

Some people like to get complicated with recipes like ratatouille, but not me. My approach has always been to create recipes and make dishes that taste fancy, while remaining simple to prepare and serve. With culinary shortcuts and by using certain easy techniques in vegan cooking, I am able to create complex flavors without getting too complicated in the kitchen. Let's face it: eating and savoring the food that you make, with your guests, is a much more enjoyable use of your time than spending way too many hours in food preparation. This ratatouille recipe tastes so flavorful, and better yet, it pretty much makes itself once you let it simmer. It is also one of those recipes that will fill your house with wonderful and delicious scents. Be careful—you might attract the whole neighborhood with this one!

3 tablespoons extra-virgin olive oil	1 small red sweet bell pepper, chopped
7 garlic cloves, chopped	1 small yellow sweet bell pepper, chopped
2 large onion, chopped	
1 tablespoon sugar	1 (6-ounce) can tomato paste
¼ cup red wine	1 cup water
1 small green squash zucchini, peeled and cubed	2 teaspoons dried parsley
5 small yellow squash zucchini, peeled and cubed	1 teaspoon dried basil
	½ teaspoon dried Italian seasoning
1 large eggplant, peeled and cubed	Salt and pepper, to taste

In a large stockpot, sauté garlic and onions in olive oil on low heat for 5 minutes, then stir in sugar and continue to caramelize on low heat, stirring occasionally until garlic and onions are translucent.

Deglaze pan with wine. Add the remaining ingredients to pan and mix thoroughly. Simmer on low heat for 1 hour, stirring occasionally, until all vegetables are tender and fully cooked. Serve with crusty French bread.

Baked Macaroni and Cheese

Serves 6-8

This is probably my single most favorite way to eat pasta…who am I kidding, I love *all* pasta each and every single way it is prepared! This baked macaroni and cheese *is* exquisite, though—truly.

1 pound dry elbow or small shell pasta
¼ cup vegan butter
2 cups plain vegan milk
¼ cup vegan cream cheese
1 teaspoon onion powder
¼ teaspoon garlic powder
1 teaspoon mustard powder

¼ teaspoon ground turmeric
2 cups vegan cheddar cheese, shredded
1 tablespoon nutritional yeast (optional)
1 cup bread crumbs, any style
Olive oil cooking spray
Salt and pepper, to taste

Preheat oven to 350° and grease a 9 x 13-inch baking dish. Boil pasta according to package directions, until tender.

In a medium saucepan on low heat, combine butter, milk, cream cheese, onion powder, garlic powder, mustard and turmeric; heat for 3–5 minutes, whisking constantly. Whisk in 1 cup cheddar cheese and simmer, stirring constantly, until cheese is melted and combined well. Season cheese sauce with salt and pepper to taste.

In a large mixing bowl, combine cheese sauce, cooked pasta, remaining 1 cup of cheddar cheese and nutritional yeast (if using). Pour pasta into greased baking dish and spread evenly. Top macaroni with breadcrumbs and spray generously with olive oil spray. Bake uncovered for 30 minutes, or until cheese is melty and topping is golden brown.

Italian Wedding Soup

Makes 8–10 servings

Despite the name, this is not a soup just made for Italian weddings. It can be, but the name originates from the marriage of the flavors, specifically the broth and the spinach greens. Traditionally, this soup is made with chicken broth and can be found on menus at most Italian restaurants. I have seen Italian wedding soup made in many different ways depending on the region that the soup maker grew up in; I have even seen a similar recipe for a Spanish wedding soup. This is my take on Italian wedding soup, based closely on the way I remember it as a child and without using any animal products. I think I do the recipe justice; I have even served this to my Italian family members who absolutely love my version. Although I mostly use vegetable broth in this soup, I have used vegan "chicken" broth before and it comes out well. That said, it is not as readily available the way vegetable broth is, so I tend to stick with this recipe unless I happen across "chicken" broth that's vegan-friendly.

---

6 cups vegetable broth
1 (10-ounce) package frozen spinach, thawed and chopped
2 large onions, chopped
3 garlic cloves, minced
2 cups carrots, peeled and chopped
½ cup celery, finely chopped

1 pound frozen vegan meatballs
1 pound vegan chicken strips, chopped
2 tablespoons fresh parsley, chopped
½ cup small dry pasta (orzo or small shells work great)
Salt and pepper, to taste

In a large stockpot over medium heat, combine broth, spinach, onions, garlic, carrots, celery; bring to a gentle boil then simmer on low-medium heat. Add "meatballs", "chicken", parsley, salt and pepper to taste; mix well and let simmer for 10 minutes.

Reduce heat to a low simmer and add dry pasta. Cook for 30 minutes longer, stirring occasionally. Soup is ready when pasta and vegetables are tender. Serve with Italian bread if desired.

Italian Stuffed Peppers

Serves 4

This recipe for stuffed peppers is a veganized version of the classic Italian dish that my grandmother made, as did her mother before her, and so on. I stuck with the same idea and the same flavors, while making the recipe my own. I think the Italian Nanas would be proud.

4 large bell peppers, any color
2 tablespoons extra-virgin olive oil
1 large onion, chopped
1 garlic clove, minced
1 pound vegan beef crumbles
½ cup cooked rice, white or brown
1 teaspoon dried Italian seasoning

3 tablespoons vegan parmesan, grated
1½ cups vegan mozzarella cheese, shredded
2 cups tomato marinara sauce
Salt and pepper, to taste

Preheat oven to 350°F and grease a square baking dish. Cut across the top of each bell pepper, removing the stem and a little flesh around it. Remove the seeds and discard. Place peppers in greased baking dish.

In a large skillet on medium heat, sauté onions and garlic in 1 tablespoon of olive oil, until fragrant. Add crumbles and cook until browned. Remove from heat and stir in rice, Italian seasoning, parmesan cheese, 1 cup mozzarella cheese shreds and 1 cup marinara sauce; season with salt and pepper to taste. Spoon this filling into bell peppers, packing filling down into the peppers by gently pushing filling down as you stuff them. Top peppers with 1 cup of marinara sauce, ½ cup of mozzarella shreds, and drizzle with 1 tablespoon of olive oil. Bake covered for 30 minutes, then bake for an additional 10–15 minutes uncovered, until bell peppers are tender and cheese on top is melted.

Franks, Beans and Biscuits Bake

Makes 6 servings

I came up with this recipe one day when, while making my usual vegan franks and beans recipe, the thought occurred to me that the meal was lacking in something. But what could it be? Biscuits, of course! At first, I would use store-bought crescent roll dough, but before long I started using my own biscuit recipe and I haven't looked back. This recipe will remain unchanged in my household because it is such an incredible hit. This meal can be made quickly and it is one that can be enjoyed at any time of year. I have made this to be served outside for an outdoor patio dinner, for cookouts, and countless times in the fall or winter, so it really does work well for any occasion.

2 cups all-purpose flour
1 tablespoon baking powder
½ teaspoon salt
½ cup extra-virgin olive oil
½ cup soy (or other vegan) milk
1 (28-ounce) can vegan baked beans
4 vegan hotdogs, cut into chunks
1 (7-ounce) package vegan bacon, chopped

1 small onion, finely chopped
¼ teaspoon garlic powder
¼ cup ketchup
2 tablespoons brown sugar
1 cup vegan cheese (cheddar, mozzarella or any flavor), shredded

Preheat oven to 350°F and grease a 9 x 13-inch baking dish. In a large mixing bowl, combine flour, baking powder and salt. Cut in olive oil and milk to dry mixture; knead dough with clean hands and set aside.

In a large skillet on medium heat, combine beans, hotdogs, "bacon", onion, garlic powder, ketchup and brown sugar; bring to a boil and simmer for 5 minutes while stirring constantly. Remove from heat, stir in shredded cheese and immediately transfer to greased baking dish. Roll out biscuit dough and, using a biscuit cutter, form 10 biscuits. Top bean mixture with biscuits. Bake covered for 40 minutes, baking for an additional 10 minutes uncovered, or until biscuits on top are flaky and thoroughly cooked. Let casserole set for 10 minutes before serving.

Slow Cooker Cabbage Soup

Serves 4-6

On a cold, rainy day, I crave soup like this cabbage soup, with delicious bread to dip in the broth. Not only is it warm and comforting, it also carries some benefits with it. Experts says that cabbage is an excellent source of vitamin B-6, vitamin K and vitamin C.

3 tablespoons vegan butter
2 garlic cloves, minced
1 small onion, chopped
1 small head cabbage, destemmed and shredded
½ cup carrots, chopped
1 (12-ounce) package vegan ground beef

4 cups vegetable broth
1 tablespoon sugar
1 bay leaf
⅛ teaspoon dried thyme
⅛ teaspoon dried rosemary
Salt and pepper, to taste

Place all ingredients in slow cooker and cook on high heat setting for 5 hours, or until cabbage and carrots are tender. Serve with some buttered bread if desired.

Easy Meatless Meatloaf with Sweet Glaze Topping

Makes 4-6 servings

I like to create recipes for use with any vegan product the user can find; however, this is one of the only recipes where I will recommend a specific brand. I find that Lightlife Gimme Lean vegan ground beef works best in this meatloaf. Having made vegan meatloaf many times, sometimes using lentils and sometimes adding rice or cheese to the mixture, this specific recipe is hands down the closest you can get if your goal is to make a classic meatloaf.

1 (14-ounce) package vegan ground beef, sticky textured (like Lightlife Gimme Lean)	1 cup bread crumbs, any style
	⅓ cup ketchup
2 tablespoons ground flaxseed mixed with 1 tablespoon water	1 tablespoon brown sugar
	1 tablespoon maple syrup
1 small onion, finely chopped	1 tablespoon Dijon mustard
1 garlic clove, minced	Salt and pepper, to taste

Preheat oven to 350°F and grease a 5 x 9-inch loaf pan. In a large bowl, combine vegan beef, flaxseed water mixture, onion, garlic, bread crumbs, salt and pepper to taste; when mixed well, form evenly into loaf pan.

In a small mixing bowl, whisk together ketchup, brown sugar, maple syrup and mustard to make glaze. Pour glaze over top of meatloaf and bake covered for 40 minutes. Uncover and bake for an additional 15–20 minutes.

Mark Hapka's Curry Peanut Lentil Loaf

Makes 6–8 servings

When doing an online search for my vegetarian friend, the dreamboat Mark Hapka, it's no surprise that his name and the word "shirtless" come up in the results before you even finish typing his full name! Mark Hapka is a talented actor who's been all over the television, movie and red carpet scene (perhaps you know him as the super-hunky Nathan on *Days of Our Lives*), but did you know he is also a plant-based-eating, animal-loving activist?

Creating recipes is easy for Mark because his favorite flavors are so versatile. Mark is a fan of anything high protein (like seitan and lentils), but he also loves aromatic foods like garlic or the flavors in Thai cuisine. So, for him I have created this amazing lentil loaf that is sort of Thai inspired. Having a dish that is full of lean vegan protein, has lots of fiber, is bursting with flavor, and can be beautifully presented while also being easy to prepare, is perfect for a busy movie star—or anyone else with a busy schedule who wants something gourmet without it being complicated. This protein-packed lentil loaf is also the perfect main dish to follow a gym session (along with a side dish or two). For more of Mark, I definitely recommend following him on Twitter and Instagram (username @ MarkHapka). He is a kind, smart and funny guy with a wonderful personality, so you'll enjoy his posts for sure!

1 medium onion, chopped	¼ teaspoon ground ginger
2 garlic cloves, minced	3 tablespoons ketchup
1 tablespoon extra-virgin olive oil	1 teaspoon Dijon mustard
2 cups cooked lentils	2 tablespoons brown sugar
½ cup bread crumbs	1 teaspoon pure maple syrup
2 tablespoons creamy peanut butter	1 tablespoon soy sauce
1 teaspoon dried basil	¼ teaspoon curry powder
1 teaspoon curry powder	Salt, to taste

Preheat oven to 350°F and grease a 5 x 9-inch loaf pan. In a blender or food processor, puree onion, garlic and olive oil, then add to a large mixing bowl. Mix in cooked lentils, bread crumbs, peanut butter, basil, 1 teaspoon curry powder, ginger and salt to taste, and combine well. Spread lentil mixture into greased loaf pan.

In a small mixing bowl, combine ketchup, mustard, brown sugar, maple syrup, soy sauce, ¼ teaspoon of curry powder and salt to taste to make a glaze. Spread glaze evenly on top of the lentil loaf. Cover and bake for 30 minutes then uncover and bake for an additional 15–20 minutes longer.

Easiest Ever "Beef", Squash and Tomato Stew

Serves 4

Recipes for meals that can be thrown together and practically "cook themselves" are the best! I am a big fan of stew—an easy dish to put together that is warm and comforting and can be eaten with crusty bread, my favorite! But let's be real: the same old stew, with the same ordinary ingredients, can get boring. I created this stew with a fresh element that certainly kicks it up a notch; butternut squash is the star. The squash lends such a lovely flavor to this stew that it might just become your new favorite; it sure is mine!

1 tablespoon extra–virgin olive oil	1 (28-ounce) can crushed tomatoes
1 large onion, chopped	1 cup vegetable broth
1½ cups butternut squash, peeled and cubed	3 garlic cloves, minced
	2 tablespoons dried parsley
2 packages frozen beefless product chunks	Salt and pepper, to taste

In a large saucepan, sauté onions in olive oil until fragrant. Add butternut squash, beefless product, tomatoes, broth, garlic and dried parsley to pot; stir. Bring stew to a boil, then simmer on low for 1 hour. Stir occasionally. Can be served with crusty bread or with breadsticks.

Sweet Potato Shepherd's Pie

Makes 8 servings

I love that this recipe can either be thrown together, with the sweet potato topping just plopped and spread on top, or you can make it fancy by piping it on with a pastry bag and decorative frosting tip. If you have the piping bags and decorating tips handy, designing the top of the casserole won't take much more time or effort; literally any elegant or ornate design pattern that you can think up can be used to turn this ordinary shepherd's pie into a culinary masterpiece, seriously impressing your guests. However, this is unnecessary if you are short on time; the taste of this shepherd's pie is extraordinary enough.

2 tablespoons extra-virgin olive oil
1 large onion, chopped
1 garlic clove, minced
1 pound vegan beef crumbles
2 tablespoons all-purpose flour
2 cups vegetable broth
½ (15-ounce) block firm tofu, drained and pureed
1 teaspoon dried Italian seasoning

½ cup frozen sweet corn
½ cup frozen green peas
4 cups cooked sweet potato mash, fresh or canned
¼ cup vegan butter, melted
1 tablespoon maple syrup
¼ teaspoon nutmeg
Salt and pepper, to taste

Preheat oven to 375°F and grease a 9 x 13-inch baking dish. In a large saucepan on medium heat, sauté onion and garlic in olive oil until fragrant. Add "beef" crumbles to pan and sauté, stirring frequently, until browned. Sprinkle flour over "beef" and stir constantly until flour is lightly toasted, then slowly stir in broth. Add tofu puree, Italian seasoning, corn, peas, salt and pepper to taste, to pan and sauté for 5 minutes, stirring frequently. Carefully pour "beef" and vegetable mixture into greased baking dish.

In a blender or food processor, combine sweet potato , melted butter, maple syrup, nutmeg, salt and pepper to taste; blend until smooth. Spread or pipe sweet potato mixture on top of casserole. Bake uncovered for 35–40 minutes. Let casserole sit for about 10 minutes before serving.

"Chicken" Pot Pie

Makes 10 servings

Pot pie was an occasional dinner option when I was growing up, though most of the time we ate the little frozen ones from the box that my mom just had to bake and serve. Yet that was a real treat for us; my brother and I grew up with an Italian mother who cooked a lot of our meals from scratch, so it was really special when we were served those little pot pies. As a kid, I had no idea about how unhealthy that food was and how cruel the animal products industry is; and in all honesty, what I really liked about the pot pies was the crust. So, when I created this large vegan casserole version, I focused on making the crust taste similar to what I remembered and enjoyed as a kid.

3½ cups all-purpose flour
2 teaspoons salt
½ teaspoon black pepper
½ tablespoon sugar
1 cup vegan butter
½ cup water
2 tablespoons extra-virgin olive oil
½ cup onion, finely chopped

1 garlic clove, minced
½ cup celery, finely chopped
2 cups vegetable stock
1 cup plain vegan milk
1 cup frozen mixed vegetable
1 cup vegan chicken strips, chopped
½ teaspoon dried Italian seasoning
Salt and pepper, to taste

Preheat oven to 375°F and generously grease a 9 x 13-inch baking dish. In a large mixing bowl, combine 3 cups of flour, 2 teaspoons salt, ½ teaspoon black pepper and sugar; cut in butter and mix in water. Knead dough and form into two evenly-sized balls; wrap and refrigerate one of the balls while you make pot pie filling.

With the other ball of dough, roll out on a lightly floured surface and press in bottom and up sides of greased baking dish; bake for 10 minutes or until dough is cooked, then remove from oven.

In a large saucepan on medium heat, sauté onion, garlic and celery until tender. Stir in ½ cup of flour and sauté, stirring constantly, until flour is slightly toasted. Stir in vegetable stock and milk. Add mixed vegetables, "chicken", Italian seasoning, salt and pepper to saucepan; cook stirring frequently until mixture has thickened. Carefully pour contents of saucepan in baking pan, over top of bottom cooked dough crust layer.

Take remaining dough ball and roll out on a lightly floured surface, to size of baking dish, and place on top of pot pie. With a fork, press down around pot pie to crimp and seal, then poke a few holes on top of pie to vent. Bake covered for 30 minutes, then uncovered for last 10 minutes of baking. Let pot pie sit for 10 minutes before serving.

Stuffing Biscuits, page 158

Sides

We can't always make every meal a giant jumble of every food group (though that would make life easier!) We *do* have to make side dishes from time to time. Personally, I like making a main protein like tofu with one or more side dishes because I think variety is fun.

In this section, we'll highlight an amazing collection of side dishes, including some of my absolute favorites, as well as an assortment of options to pair beautifully with any number of dishes.

Stuffing Biscuits

Makes approximately 10 biscuits

These biscuits have always reminded me of comfort food and the holidays, but it can be made alongside any meal, at any time! It is a great recipe for when you want to serve something bread-like as a side, be it with a roast or a soup, but don't feel like making stuffing. This is also a more chic way to serve stuffing, as it is easy to make, more compact, and effortless to eat, all while being super impressive to your guests.

Additionally, if you make meals for children who don't tend to like eating stuffing but who *do* prefer bread, rolls, or biscuits, try making these stuffing biscuits for them. With such simple, stress-free preparation and a pick-up-and-eat way to enjoy stuffing, these biscuits are sure to be as much of a crowd-pleaser in your home as they are in mine!

¼ cup flaxseed, ground
¾ cup plain soy or almond milk
4 cups cubed bread, any kind
2 tablespoons vegan butter
1 small onion, finely chopped
½ cup celery, finely chopped

4 strips vegan bacon, chopped
¼ cup vegetable stock
1 teaspoon dried sage
1 teaspoon dried parsley
Salt and pepper, to taste

Preheat oven to 425°F. Line a baking sheet with high temperature resistant parchment paper and grease lightly. Combine flaxseed and milk in a large mixing bowl; add bread cubes and toss. Let bread soak up nearly all the liquid and set aside.

In a frying pan on medium heat, sauté onion and celery in butter until very soft, stirring frequently. Add bacon and sauté until browned; allow mixture to cool enough to handle safely. Add bacon mixture to bread and add remaining ingredients to mixing bowl. With clean hands, combine and roll into large balls. Bake for 20 minutes or until biscuits are golden brown.

Potato Salad

Makes 6 servings

I love a deliciously creamy potato salad, and so it really bugs me when people try to serve vegan potato salad with a little vinegar. You might as well put a handful of grass on a plate and call it a day! I consider potato salad that is nothing but potatoes with some clear, vinegar-based dressing to be a personal insult; us vegans like to enjoy our food as much as anyone else! We like our food to taste flavorful, not bland.

With that in mind, this potato salad recipe is meant to demonstrate how *I* like to enjoy this classic side dish. Feel free to bring this dish to the next cookout that you're invited to; I doubt that anyone will ever guess that it is vegan!

4 cups potatoes, peeled, cubed and cooked	1 cup celery, finely chopped
¾ cup vegan mayonnaise	1 small onion, finely chopped
	Salt and pepper, to taste

Mix all ingredients together in a large mixing bowl. Refrigerate until ready to serve.

Hollandaise Sauce

Serves 4-6

Having never personally seen a decent vegan hollandaise sauce, and doubting whether one even exists, I felt compelled to create one of my own. This is another recipe that calls for that magic ingredient, black salt powder. The addition of this one ingredient lends an egg-like flavor to your sauce.

Hollandaise sauce is commonly used on eggs Benedict; however, this sauce be used in many other ways, as well. In addition to making your own eggs Benedict with tofu and using this sauce, you can also drizzle it over the top of steamed vegetables like asparagus or green beans. This is a delicious sauce to use a bunch of different ways, so get creative!

½ (8-ounce) container vegan cream cheese
2 tablespoons ripe avocado, pureed (use the yellow flesh part if possible)

1 tablespoon fresh lemon juice
Black salt powder, to taste

In a saucepan on low heat, whisk cream cheese and avocado together while gradually adding lemon juice and black salt powder. Continue to whisk sauce constantly on low heat until thick, well combined and heated thoroughly. Use this sauce to pour on vegetables, as a dipping sauce, or in any recipe that calls for hollandaise.

Creamy Butternut Squash

Makes 4 servings

I find the combination of butternut squash with a creamy texture to be exceptionally delightful. This dish was the result of an experiment, using a new method of preparing butternut squash that I'd never tried before. When I played around with it this way and came up with this recipe, I was really pleased with the result.

This side dish goes perfectly during the autumn and winter holidays alongside a vegan roast, or even in the spring and summer as a compliment for a nice tofu main dish.

3 cups butternut squash, peeled and cubed
2 tablespoons vegan butter
½ (8-ounce) container vegan cream cheese

2 tablespoons plain vegan milk
¼ cup onion, minced
Salt and pepper, to taste

Preheat oven to 400°F and grease a large baking dish. In a large saucepan, boil squash in water until tender, about 15 minutes. Drain squash and mash. Add butter, cream cheese, milk and onion to the mashed squash. Season squash with salt and pepper to taste. Transfer mixture to greased baking dish. Cover and bake for 20 minutes.

Roasted Brussels Sprouts
with Sweet and Tangy Curry Drizzle

Serves 4–6

There are as many different types of curries as there are ways to prepare them, whether in the form of a sauce, powder, or paste. I choose to use madras curry powder in this recipe for the drizzle, because I find that it pairs well with the sweetness from the maple syrup and I *love* what the curry sauce contributes to the Brussels sprouts.

Madras curry powder results in a slightly spicy curry, so if you are one who doesn't really care for flavorful heat or are serving to guests whose preferences you are unsure about, you can always opt for a sweeter curry, or else one that is very mild. That said madras curry is far from the hottest curry that I have ever tasted and in my opinion it melds perfectly in this recipe. If you don't love spicy foods, you may want to add less and taste as you season, until you get the flavor just right for you.

1 (16-ounce) package frozen Brussels sprouts	1 tablespoon maple syrup
2 tablespoons extra-virgin olive oil	1 tablespoon soy sauce
4 tablespoons vegan mayonnaise	½ teaspoon madras curry powder
1 teaspoon Dijon mustard	Salt and pepper, to taste

Preheat oven to 400°F. Place Brussels sprouts in a baking dish and toss with olive oil until well-coated. Sprinkle with salt and pepper and then toss again. Bake for 45–50 minutes, turning once halfway through roasting. Bake Brussels sprouts until tender, cooked thoroughly and roasted to your desired doneness.

In a small mixing bowl, whisk together mayonnaise, Dijon mustard, maple syrup, soy sauce and curry powder to make a drizzle sauce. Drizzle sauce over Brussels sprouts and serve.

Sausage Gravy

Serves 8

You just might fall in love with this recipe. You have been warned.

Some ideas for this gravy, to get you started:

- You can pour it generously over mashed potatoes (try my recipe for Onion Ranch Mashed Potatoes on page 167)
- You can enjoy an amazing vegan biscuits and gravy meal (perhaps using my Olive Oil Biscuits recipe on page 66)
- You can pair it with your favorite vegan roast meal
- Honestly, you can use it for pretty much any situation where gravy is appropriate!

---

2 tablespoons vegan butter
1 pound frozen "beef" crumbles,
   somewhat large in size
½ cup all-purpose flour

4 cups soy milk
½ teaspoon fennel seeds
Salt and pepper, to taste

In a medium saucepan on medium heat, melt butter and sauté crumbles until lightly browned. Sprinkle flour over crumbles and stir constantly until crumbles are well-coated with flour. Gradually add in soy milk and fennel seeds while stirring continuously. Reduce heat slightly and continue to cook until gravy is bubbly and has thickened. Season gravy with salt and pepper to taste.

Onion Ranch
Mashed Potatoes
Makes 4–6 servings

If you have ever tasted something sour cream and onion flavored, you'll understand exactly what inspired me for this recipe. These are the best mashed potatoes that I've ever had the pleasure of consuming. If you like mashed potatoes or even potatoes in general, but are tired of the typical boring options on offer, this recipe may just become your new favorite. Try topping them with a bit of Sausage Gravy (page 166) for an extra-special hearty side dish.

The last two ingredients in this recipe, chives and parsley, are optional; although they do contribute slightly to the flavor, I used them because they make the side dish look really beautiful. So if you don't have these ingredients on hand, they can be omitted without sacrificing the main flavor of the dish. In fact, I have made these mashed potatoes without the garnish many times and they taste phenomenal no matter what!

8 medium baking potatoes, washed, peeled and cut into large chunks or cubes
1 teaspoon salt, to salt water
¼ cup vegan butter
¼ cup vegan mayonnaise
¼ cup vegan ranch-style dressing

½ tablespoon onion powder
1 tablespoon fresh chives, finely chopped (optional for garnish)
2 tablespoons fresh parsley, finely chopped (optional for garnish)
Salt and pepper, to taste

Fill a large pot with enough water to cover potatoes (about halfway). Add potatoes and salt the water by adding 1 teaspoon of salt to the pot. Bring to a boil and boil potatoes until they are very tender, approximately 20 minutes. Drain and return potatoes back to pot. Mash the potatoes. Add butter, mayonnaise, dressing, and onion powder to mashed potatoes; mix well. Season with salt and pepper to taste. Garnish with fresh chives and parsley if desired.

Maple Glazed Carrots

Serves 6–8

I came up with this recipe on a whim, when I found myself hosting guests unexpectedly and needed a side dish for dinner. I hadn't prepared, so I was looking for a vegetable side that I could whip up quickly, but which would also impress my unanticipated guests. I was able to easily prepare this side, all while chatting with my friends in the kitchen and without giving it much thought at all. That's how laid back this recipe truly is.

3 tablespoons vegan butter
½ small onion, chopped
1 teaspoon dried parsley
8 medium carrots, peeled and
    quartered

¼ cup vegetable stock
¼ cup maple syrup

In a large frying pan on medium heat, melt butter and sauté onion and parsley until onion is tender. Stir carrots and maple syrup in pan; reduce heat to medium-low. Cover and cook until carrots are tender, stirring occasionally.

Cranberry Sauce

Of all the recipes that I make, I enjoy making this cranberry sauce most of all. I love the transformation that these four simple ingredients undergo, as the fresh cranberries turn into a jelled sauce. Not to mention, it's awesome once you realize that you no longer have to purchase cranberry sauce in a can! When you can make a fresh cranberry sauce that is as simple to make as it is incredibly tasty, why would you ever compromise for store-bought sauce? This cranberry sauce can be used during fall and winter holidays alongside a roast meal or on vegan turkey sandwiches, or with any dish that goes well with this type of sauce.

You will notice that I have included some coconut sugar in this recipe. While I like the flavor it lends to the cranberry sauce, if you do not have coconut sugar on hand you can substitute it for an equal amount of regular sugar.

---

2 (12-ounce) packages fresh
   cranberries, washed
1½ cups sugar

½ cup coconut sugar
2 cups cold water

In a large saucepan, combine all ingredients and bring to a boil. Allow to rapid boil for about 5 minutes, stirring occasionally. Reduce to a low simmer, stirring occasionally, for about 10 minutes or until all cranberries have "popped". Allow to cool slightly before serving, if you are serving it warm. If you are serving a chilled sauce, refrigerate until you are ready to use.

Garlic and Caper
Roasted Cauliflower

Makes 4–6 servings

When a friend of mine mentioned that they had liked garlic roasted cauliflower for years, but had recently grown tired of the same old ordinary taste, I was struck with inspiration. I had a jar of delicious capers in my refrigerator, and so I decided to make this side dish while my friend was visiting. This was such a hit that it officially renewed his faith in garlic roasted cauliflower!

3 tablespoons vegan butter	1 tablespoon fresh lemon juice
7 garlic cloves, chopped	1 large cauliflower head, broken into
2 tablespoons capers, drained and	florets
chopped	1 tablespoon extra-virgin olive oil
1 tablespoon dried parsley	Salt and pepper, to taste

Preheat oven to 400°F. In a small saucepan, melt butter on low heat and add garlic. Sauté garlic until tender, stirring occasionally.

Remove pan from heat and stir in capers, parsley and lemon juice; set aside. Grease a baking sheet and evenly distribute cauliflower florets on it. Pour garlic caper sauce from saucepan, over cauliflower florets. Drizzle olive oil over florets and season with salt and pepper to taste. Bake for 30–40 minutes, turning florets with a wooden spoon halfway thru baking and rotating the baking sheet once, until tender and lightly browned.

Creamy Old Fashioned Coleslaw

Makes 6–8 servings

1 (16-ounce) bag of prepared coleslaw starter (shredded cabbage and carrots)	½ cup vegan mayonnaise
½ cup plain vegan milk	1 tablespoon vinegar
¼ cup vegan butter, melted	1 tablespoon sugar
	Salt and pepper, to taste

In a large mixing bowl, place coleslaw, cabbage, and carrots and set aside. In a medium mixing bowl, whisk together milk, butter, mayonnaise, vinegar, sugar, salt and pepper to taste; pour over coleslaw vegetables and toss until combined very well. Refrigerate until ready to serve.

Pan Fried
Rustic Style Cabbage

Serves 4-6

For a long time, cabbage soup and stuffed cabbage were my mainstay cabbage dishes. It wasn't until I started to really expand my cabbage game that I realized just how sad it was that I was limiting myself to just those two recipes.

Here is my absolute favorite cabbage recipe ever! This side dish is so good that you will probably turn anyone who eats it into a bona fide cabbage lover.

1 small cabbage head, sliced and with stem removed	2 teaspoon onion powder
2 tablespoons extra-virgin olive oil	1 tablespoons sugar
2 teaspoon garlic powder	¼ vegan butter
	Salt and pepper, to taste

In a large saucepan on medium heat, sauté cabbage in olive oil until slightly tender, then add garlic powder, onion powder and sugar; stir well. Pan fry for 5 minutes, stirring often. Add butter and continue to cook, stirring frequently, until liquid is reduced and cabbage is very tender. Season with salt and pepper to taste.

My Brother's Bean and Beefless Side Dish

Makes 6–8 servings

My brother embraced veganism as soon as I told him about my lifestyle, and he has been very supportive. He is always the first one to tell me about any new vegan products he finds, and loves taking me to the vegan restaurants he has discovered over the years.

This particular side dish was created by my brother, and he brought it over to my house one year for the holidays. I adored the flavors and ate so much of it that he began to bring it over every year after that! He makes a lot of vegan food, but this is my favorite one. With help from my sister-in-law, he has revised the recipe to be included in this cookbook, and I am so thankful. I hope you enjoy making it as much as I do!

½ cup brown sugar
½ cup ketchup
¼ cup white vinegar
1 tablespoon raw blue agave
½ teaspoon smoked paprika
½ teaspoon garlic powder
½ teaspoon onion powder

1 (15.5-ounce) can chickpeas, drained
1 (10-ounce) can black beans
1 (16-ounce) package frozen sweet corn
1 (9-ounce) package beefless tips
Salt and pepper, to taste

In a large sauce pan on low heat, whisk together brown sugar, ketchup, white vinegar and agave. Stir in paprika, garlic powder, onion powder and bring to a gentle boil, mixing constantly. Add chickpeas, black beans, frozen corn and beefless tips to the pan and stir. Raise heat to medium and continue cooking, stirring often, for about 15 minutes. Season with salt and pepper to taste. Remove from heat and let rest for 5 minutes before serving.

Green Bean Casserole
Makes 4–6 servings

Numerous people have told me that green bean casserole is something they long to get in a vegan version, but it is nearly impossible to find it in any vegan restaurants. No surprise; it's just as difficult to find a decent recipe for it, since the traditional dish calls for cream of mushroom soup. Too many of my fellow vegans have given up on being able to make this side dish in an easy manner, the way non-vegans can.

It is for this reason that I created this straightforward recipe, so that everyone can enjoy a vegan green bean casserole alongside their holiday meals or as an interesting addition to their everyday menu!

1 (4-ounce) can mushrooms (pieces and stems), drained	¼ cup vegetable stock
1 tablespoon vegan butter, melted	⅛ teaspoon dried thyme
½ cup vegan cream (creamer for coffee or thick soy milk can be used)	2 (14.5-ounce) cans cut green beans, drained
	¼ cup plain vegan milk
1 tablespoon all-purpose flour	1⅓ cup vegan French fried onions
	Salt and pepper, to taste

Preheat oven 350°F and grease a 1.5 quart casserole dish. In a blender or food processor, blend mushrooms, melted butter, cream, flour, vegetable stock, thyme, salt and pepper to taste, until smooth.

In a large mixing bowl, combine creamy mushroom mixture, green beans and half the fried onions. Spread evenly in greased baking dish. Cover and bake for 30 minutes. Carefully stir casserole and top with the remaining fried onions. Bake for an additional 5 minutes or until top of casserole is golden brown.

Nutty Brown Sugar
Brussels Sprouts
Serves 2–4

The thing that makes this side dish so special to me is the way the Brussels sprouts are being joined with sweetness as well as almonds and walnuts—not typically what comes to mind when thinking about the preparation Brussels sprouts. But it works, it really does; I make this recipe throughout the year, and I especially love serving it during fall or winter holidays because the flavors unite so well.

1 (10-ounce) package fresh Brussels sprouts	¼ cup walnuts, chopped
3 tablespoons vegan butter	1 tablespoon brown sugar
¼ cup almonds, chopped	⅛ teaspoon ground nutmeg
	Salt and pepper, to taste

In a large saucepan, boil Brussels sprouts until tender, about 15–20 minutes. Drain Brussels sprouts, and then transfer to a serving dish. In a small saucepan, combine butter, almonds, walnuts, brown sugar and nutmeg. Whisk constantly on low heat, bring to a boil, and remove sauce from heat. Pour sauce over Brussels sprouts and serve.

Vegan Dark Chocolate
Peanut Butter Blossoms,
page 182

Sweets and Treats

Vegan sweets are my favorite treats. As the former owner and head pastry chef of a vegan bakery, Dirty Vegan Foods, vegan baking holds a special place in my heart. I love the science of baking as it melds with the art of creating dessert recipes.

The recipes in this next section will surely knock the socks off of anyone who eats them!

Vegan Dark Chocolate Peanut Butter Blossoms

Makes 3 dozen cookies

Growing up, these cookies were always out on the cookie trays, no matter what the occasion. I have always wanted to find a way to make them vegan; however, the recipe calls for a specific shaped candy that is difficult to find in vegan form.

Being a huge lover of dark chocolate, it made sense for me to finally recreate the recipe I remembered from when I was a kid, but with dark chocolate squares. Like every other vegan food item that I make, I can honestly say that I like them way better this way!

½ cup creamy peanut butter
½ cup vegan butter
½ cup brown sugar
¼ cup coconut sugar
¼ cup vegan milk
1 teaspoon vanilla
2 cups all-purpose flour

1 teaspoon baking soda
½ teaspoon salt
3 tablespoons cane sugar, for tops of cookies (optional)
36 small vegan dark chocolate squares

Preheat oven to 375°F. Line three baking sheets with high temperature resistant parchment paper. With a mixer, beat together peanut butter, butter, brown sugar, coconut sugar, milk and vanilla.

In a large mixing bowl, combine flour, baking soda and salt. Mix butter mixture together with flour mixture. Roll balls of dough about 1 tablespoon in size to form cookies and gently press the tops down in cane sugar. If some of the dough appears crumbly, it is okay; just press it together to form the proper shape.

Arrange cookies on baking sheet, evenly spaced at least one inch apart. Bake for 9 minutes; upon removing from oven, immediately and carefully press a small square of chocolate into the top of each cookie.

This recipe can also be made with almond butter in place of peanut butter.

Mini Cannoli Bites

Makes 15 bites

Growing up in a small Italian town in Connecticut, the smell of cannoli wafting through the air was a constant, especially in the center of town where all the Italian bakeries resided.

When I became vegan, I found that I missed the Italian pastries of my childhood most of all. While I did not miss the animal products, I missed the flavors and longed to make some type of vegan cannoli recipe.

These bites bring me back to another time, and they really couldn't be any easier, with pre-made fillo shells and simple ingredients ensuring no mess and no stress.

1 (1.9-ounce) package vegan precooked mini fillo dough shells, 15 count
½ (8-ounce) container vegan cream cheese
2 tablespoons vegan vanilla yogurt

1 tablespoon maple syrup
½ teaspoon fresh orange zest
⅛ teaspoon ground cinnamon
⅛ cup vegan mini semi-sweet chocolate chips

On a serving tray, arrange mini fillo shells and prepare a pastry bag with a tip; set both aside.

In a medium mixing bowl, mix together cream cheese, yogurt, maple syrup, orange zest and cinnamon until smooth and combined well. Pipe cannoli filling evenly into each mini fillo cup until all filling is gone. Sprinkle mini chocolate chips on top of each cannoli cup. Refrigerate until ready to serve.

For best results, chill for at least one hour before serving.

Kiddo Approved
Strawberry Banana Milkshake
Makes 2–3 milkshakes

I asked my kiddo what her favorite flavor of milkshake was, and this is what she told me. We then proceeded to make this strawberry banana milkshake, and as soon as I got her seal of approval I knew it was ready for me to share with the world. (This milkshake also got a thumbs up and a, "This is delicious!" for those who were wondering).

Use extra ripe bananas and good quality strawberries for the best flavor.

2 ripe bananas
1 cup frozen strawberries
2 cups vanilla soy milk

4 scoops vanilla ice cream
Whipped topping and sliced fresh
   strawberries, for garnish (optional)

In a blender, blend bananas, frozen strawberries, milk and ice cream. Milkshakes can be served with a dollop of whipped topping and slices of fresh strawberries on top, if desired.

Choconilla Peanut Butter Milkshake for One

Serves 1

There is something downright divine about the combination of chocolate and peanut butter. Try making this delicious milkshake on those days that the chocolate and peanut butter cravings are too real to resist!

½ cup chocolate almond or soy milk
¼ cup vanilla almond or soy milk
1 tablespoon vegan chocolate syrup

2 tablespoons peanut butter
2–4 scoops vegan vanilla ice cream
(depending on desired thickness)

Blend all ingredients in a blender or food processor and transfer to a tall glass. Serve with a dollop of whipped topping on top, if desired.

Buttery Almond Cookies

Makes 3 dozen cookies

These almond cookies are so amazing that you may have trouble eating just one! Some cookies are just way too easy to eat, and this cookie recipe is no exception. They are also a dainty dessert, so they are perfect for serving during tea parties or holidays. These cookies remind me of my grandmother; although her almond cookies were different in style and texture, the almond taste is very similar.

I recommend that you use pure extracts rather than imitation flavorings, to get the best results (just like my grandma did). Eating these almond cookies feels very nostalgic, and I hope that when you try them, you can create some happy feelings of your own!

½ cup vegan butter, softened
¼ cup sugar
½ cup almond slivers, chopped
1 teaspoon almond extract

¼ teaspoon vanilla extract
1 cup all-purpose flour
36 almond halves

Preheat oven to 350°F and line three baking sheets with high temperature resistant parchment paper. Cream the butter and sugar together very well. Stir in chopped almond slivers, almond extract, and finally the flour.

Roll dough into heaping teaspoon-sized balls and arrange evenly on baking sheets, spaced at least 1 inch apart. With the palm of your hand, slightly flatten each ball of dough and press an almond half into the center of each one. Bake for 8–10 minutes, or until cookies are slightly golden.

Simply the Best
Coffee Cake

Serves 8

This coffee cake is simply unlike any coffee cake that I have ever tasted. It is moist and delicious; it can be served alone after a meal, as a snack in between meals, or even for breakfast alongside a nice cup of coffee or tea.

If you have memories of coffee cake from before becoming vegan, you might just be instantly brought back to that memory after just one bite. If you have never had coffee cake before, you are in for a treat!

1 ½ cups all-purpose flour
½ cup and 2 tablespoons sugar, divided
½ teaspoon salt
2 ½ teaspoons baking powder
¼ cup vegetable shortening, softened
¾ cup vanilla flavored soy or almond milk

2 tablespoons ground flaxseed mixed with 1 ½ tablespoons water
⅓ cup brown sugar
¼ cup all-purpose flour
½ teaspoon cinnamon
3 tablespoons vegan butter

Preheat oven to 375°F and grease an 8-inch round cake pan, or similar sized pan. In a large mixing bowl, combine 1½ cups of flour, sugar, salt, baking powder, shortening, milk, and flaxseed and water mixture; mix thoroughly. Pour batter into greased cake pan.

In a medium mixing bowl, combine brown sugar, ¼ cup of flour, cinnamon and butter until crumbly and mixed well; sprinkle evenly on top of the batter. Bake for 25 minutes or until a cake tester inserted into the cake comes out cleanly when removed.

Pumpkin Pie Cheesecake
Makes 8 servings

This is a classic dish in the Gill house; my guests, whether they are vegan or not, look forward to this dessert every year during the holidays. Canned pumpkin puree is easy to find during any season, meaning it is easy to make this cake all year round.

What makes this dessert so special is the way it combines two dessert flavors into one—pumpkin pie and cheesecake. A dollop of whipped topping or a scoop of ice cream completes the ensemble, if you desire. This pie is sure to be a crowd-pleaser no matter what.

1 (9-inch) prepared graham cracker crust
1 cup canned pumpkin puree
1 (8-ounce) container vegan cream cheese
¾ (15-ounce) block form tofu, drained
1 cup sugar

3½ tablespoons all-purpose flour
¼ teaspoon baking powder
1½ teaspoons ground cinnamon
½ teaspoon ground ginger
¼ teaspoon ground nutmeg
¼ teaspoon ground allspice
Pinch of salt

Preheat oven to 350°F and have the prepared pie crust ready for use. In a food processor or blender, puree the remaining ingredients until smooth and combined well; pour into prepared pie crust.

Bake uncovered for 40 minutes or until cheesecake is wobbly in the center and the outer edges are firm with less or no jiggle. This pie will continue to cook and set even after being removed from oven. Allow to set and cool for at least 20 minutes, then cover and refrigerate until serving. Cheesecake is fully set after 4–6 hours of being chilled in refrigerator.

Amazing Apple Pie

Serves 8

I once made this for my future mother-in-law (I was only dating her son at the time), and I am convinced that it was this pie that won her over. I had just turned vegan when I first came up with this pie recipe, and I have to admit I was nervous to serve this dessert to my boyfriend's mother. Not only was I just starting out in veganism.

This apple pie recipe remains unchanged from the day that I created it. I added my own unconventional touches, like spices to the pie crust and including maple syrup in the filling. I wanted the dough to be as special as the filling, that way if you eat a bite at the end, without the filling, the crust alone tastes as beautiful as the pie does. These days, I use a fun-shaped cookie cutter to make my vent hole in the top of the crust, and place the piece of dough that I removed elsewhere on the pie as a cute finishing touch.

I hope your reaction upon taking your first bite is the same as my mother-in-law's— she raved about it being the best apple pie she had ever tasted!

Pie crust

2 cups all-purpose flour
2½ teaspoons sugar
½ teaspoon salt
½ teaspoon ground cinnamon
¼ teaspoon ground nutmeg
⅓ cup vegan butter
⅓ cup vegetable shortening
¼ cup water, use as needed according to directions

Pie filling

¼ cup brown sugar
¼ cup sugar
¼ cup all-purpose flour
½ teaspoon ground cinnamon
¼ teaspoon ground nutmeg
⅛ teaspoon ground ginger
6 cups apples, peeled, cored and thinly sliced
¼ cup maple syrup
1 tablespoon vegan butter, melted, to top pie before baking
2 teaspoons sugar, to top pie before baking

Preheat oven to 400°F and lightly grease and flour a 9-inch round pie baking dish or pan. In a large mixing bowl, combine 2 cups flour, 2½ teaspoons sugar, salt, ½ teaspoon cinnamon, and ¼ teaspoon nutmeg. Cream together butter and shortening, and then cut it into flour mixture until crumbly. Add water, 1 tablespoon at a time, and mix until you get desired dough consistency—a moistened dough that you can form with your hands.

Divide dough in half to make two dough balls. Cover and refrigerate one ball; with the other dough ball, roll it out on a lightly floured surface in a circular shape slightly larger than your pie dish. Place dough into greased and floured pie dish; if dough hangs over pie dish too much, trim the excess so that it sits at the rim edge of the dish or pan.

In a very large mixing bowl, combine brown sugar, sugar, flour, ½ teaspoon cinnamon, ¼ teaspoon nutmeg, and ⅛ teaspoon ginger. Add apples and toss, before adding maple syrup to apples and tossing again. Add apples to pie dish and spread them evenly.

Remove dough ball from refrigerator and roll out on a lightly floured surface, in a circular shape and size that will meet up with bottom crust. With a fork, crimp the top and bottom crusts to seal. Brush melted butter on top of pie and sprinkle with 2 teaspoons sugar. Make small slits in top of pie crust to vent. If desired, cover with crust shield to prevent edges from getting overcooked.

Bake for 35 minutes. Remove crust shield if using, and bake for an additional 10 minutes, or until crust is golden brown and you notice apple juices bubbling up the pie vents. Allow pie to set for 5 minutes or more, prior to serving. If desired, serve a la mode with a scoop of vegan vanilla ice cream or with a dollop of whipped topping.

Apple Crisp
Makes 6–8 servings

Apple crisp is one of those desserts that can be served after a meal or as the meal itself, as a great breakfast to enjoy with coffee or tea the next day. For that reason, I often call this dish "Breakfast Apple Pie."

Apple crisp is also the perfect sweet treat to be eaten a la mode. Try making it a few times with different varieties of apples to get a sweeter, juicier, or tarter crisp.

4 cups apples, peeled, cored and
    sliced
¾ cup brown sugar
½ cup all-purpose flour
½ cup rolled oats

1 teaspoon cinnamon
½ teaspoon nutmeg
⅛ teaspoon ginger
⅓ cup vegan butter, softened

Preheat oven to 375°F and grease a large baking dish (about 9 x 13 inches). Evenly spread apple slices in greased baking pan.

In a medium mixing bowl, combine brown sugar, flour, rolled oats, cinnamon, nutmeg and ginger to make the topping; mix well. Cut butter into flour mixture and mix until well combined and crumbly. Sprinkle topping evenly over apples. Bake for 30–40 minutes or until apples are tender and topping is golden brown. Serve spooned into bowls; if desired, top with a dollop of whipped topping or a scoop of vegan vanilla ice cream.

Chocolate Peanut Butter Banana Ice Cream Pie

Makes 8 servings

I make this ice cream pie every year during the springtime, and any other time when I want to make an impressive dessert that tastes out-of-this-world amazing while being super simple. Since I have made this pie so many times, it only takes me a matter of minutes to whip everything together.

A no-bake pie like this one is really convenient in today's busy times. It's great to make the night before, or even in the morning before work to be enjoyed that night after dinner (since it needs about 6 hours to freeze well and firm up nicely.)

½ cup creamy peanut butter
¼ cup maple syrup
1 quart vegan vanilla ice cream, softened
1 prepared graham cracker pie crust, 9 inch size
½ cup and 2 tablespoons peanuts, chopped

1 rip (but firm) banana, thinly sliced
½ cup vegan semi-sweet chocolate chips
2 tablespoons vanilla vegan soy milk
1 tablespoon coconut oil

In a large mixing bowl, cream together peanut butter and maple syrup; combine with ice cream. Spread half of ice cream mixture evenly in pie crust. Sprinkle an even layer of ¼ cup of the chopped peanuts on top of ice cream layer and arrange banana slices evenly over top of peanuts. Place in freezer while you make chocolate ganache.

In a small saucepan on low heat, melt chocolate chips, soy milk and coconut oil together, stirring frequently. When well combined, remove ganache from heat and set aside. Remove pie from freezer and pour on a layer of half of the chocolate ganache; spread remaining ice cream mixture on top of that. Lastly, sprinkle ¼ cup chopped peanuts and the last of the chocolate ganache. Sprinkle with last 2 tablespoons of chopped peanuts, cover with lid (that accompanies prepared pie crust) and freeze overnight or until firm.

My Famous Chocolate Peanut Butter Cups

Makes 3 dozen chocolate peanut butter cups

These are my famous peanut butter cups that I make for every occasion I can. As a result, I've become greatly known for my chocolate peanut butter cup making ability, and this dessert is requested quite often. Make these and watch them quickly disappear!

I have also made these sweet heavenly morsels with almond butter and they taste phenomenal either way!

1 cup creamy peanut butter	¼ teaspoon salt
¼ cup vegan butter, softened	3 cups vegan semi-sweet chocolate
½ cup powdered sugar	chips

In a medium mixing bowl, combine ½ cup peanut butter, butter, powdered sugar and salt. Form into a ball, cover and refrigerate.

In a medium saucepan on low, melt together remaining ½ cup peanut butter and chocolate chips, stirring constantly until combined well; remove from heat and set aside. Remove peanut butter mixture and divide into 36 balls, about 1 teaspoon in size. Pour melted chocolate mixture in 36 mini muffin cups/ liners, filling about ⅓ of the cup. Drop a peanut butter filling ball into each cup. Pour the remaining melted chocolate evenly into all of the 36 cups to cover the peanut butter filling, until all of the melted chocolate is gone. Refrigerate for several hours until set; for best results, refrigerate overnight.

Caramel Nut Candies

Makes 40 caramel candies

This candy recipe was born from my making caramel sauces to top ice cream and other desserts. One day, I made more of a volume of the caramel sauce and added in nuts along with the other ingredients, allowed it to cool enough to handle, and suddenly realized that what I held was exactly like soft caramel candy!

Depending on boiling times and temperatures, you can play around with this recipe to get to the exact caramel texture and hardness or softness that you desire. You can use a candy thermometer, but it is not necessary. I have made these both with and without use of the thermometer, and it came out exactly the same way. This recipe is for a caramel that is on the chewy side. You can also fold in coconut or other yummy add-ins, so get creative with it!

½ cup maple syrup
½ cup coconut oil
½ cup almond butter

½ teaspoon vanilla extract
¼ cup of your favorite nuts (walnuts or cashews work great in this candy)

Line a baking dish or pan (about 8 x 8 inches) with parchment paper (be sure that excess parchment paper comes up the sides of the pan to allow for easier removal later) and set aside. Cut 40 strips of parchment paper or waxed paper, about 3 inches long by 2 inches wide, and set aside; these will be your wrappers.

In a medium saucepan on low heat, melt all ingredients together while whisking constantly. If you are using a candy thermometer, heat the candy mixture until it reaches 240°F, the magic caramel number; if not using a thermometer, bring caramel sauce to a gentle boil and remove from heat when gently bubbling, but *before* it would begin to burn. Note that the mixture can be removed from heat fairly quickly once it starts gently boiling and all ingredients are well combined.

Remove from heat and allow it to cool for 1 minute, stirring frequently, and then transfer the caramel into the pan on top of parchment. Allow to fully cool and set in refrigerator for at least 3 hours before cutting.

Cut five rows down and eight across, cutting 40 caramel candies. Place each caramel in a wrapper and twist the ends to secure. Alternatively, you can roll into small candy balls after waiting for the caramel to cool enough to handle, and wrap them in that shape. They can even be dipped in a melted chocolate coating and set to make chocolate covered caramel nut candies!

Store in refrigerator for best result.

Ambrosia Fruit Salad

Makes 8–10 servings

If you are wondering what this dessert is all about, think refreshing fruit salad, but done Dirty Vegan style! Add some whipped topping and mini marshmallows, and you've got ambrosia salad!

This was so common when I was growing up; my grandmother made ambrosia salad for every occasion and I ate so much of it I simply *had* to veganize it!

2 cups canned pineapple chunks, drained

1 cup canned mandarin oranges, drained

½ cup maraschino cherries, drained and halved

1 cup shredded or flaked coconut

2 cups vegan mini marshmallows

1 (9-ounce) container vegan coconut whipped topping, thawed

2 tablespoons vegan sour cream

In a large mixing bowl, blend all ingredients together until well combined. Cover and chill for 1–2 hours before serving. Serve chilled for best taste.

Mini Cannoli Bites, page 183

Conclusion

I hope that this cookbook has inspired you in some way. Whether you are incorporating vegan meals into your diet for the sake of the animals, to lessen the unfavorable effects on the environment, or even for health reasons, you have the opportunity to make a giant impact in a positive way.

Veganism is more than just the compassionate way to go. It's the lifestyle choice that has the greatest overall benefit, positively touching the lives of those who practice it, saving the lives of animals even as we relieve some of the eco-burden of our planet. Experts say that eating even one plant-based meal per week—a Meatless Monday, for example—is very helpful to human health, Mother Nature, and of course our animal friends.

Bottom line? The more you eat vegan, the better! So go ahead and go vegan to your heart's content; I won't stop you! And for now—until the next book—The Dirty Vegan is signing off.

Happy cooking to you, Friends.

Avocado and "Bacon" Cheesy Cheddar Bread Ring, page 33

Acknowledgements

There are so many people who help me and inspire me, and who continue to do so throughout my vegan life's journey. Thank you, from the bottom of my heart, to everyone who assisted in making this book and this beautiful vegan life possible. In no particular order, I would like to give the most heartfelt thanks to:

My daughter, S, who inspired me to take my writing and activism further by writing this book. You motivate me every second of every day to be the best version of myself possible. I wanted you to see me do this, to know that women can do anything we set our minds to. I wanted you to watch me fulfill one of my dreams, so that you'll know everything we can dream up is possible, and can absolutely be done. Always follow your dreams, no matter the obstacles, no matter who tells you it cannot be done—let your heart and your dreams be your guide. I appreciate your patience and helpfulness during the cookbook creating process. Also, thank you for the contribution of your wonderful milkshake recipe; now, vegan kiddos from around the globe can enjoy it, too! I am so proud of you, and I love you so much.

To my husband, J, who has been with me through my entire journey of getting to The Dirty Vegan. You have supported and inspired me the entire way. There was never any resistance, no matter how foreign these new ideas were to you, those many years ago. You happily took the ride right along with me. You are always right alongside me, as my partner, and no matter how grandiose my ideas seem, you work so hard to help my dreams come true. Thank you for all of your help and thank you for always encouraging my aspirations, ever since 2003. I love and appreciate you.

Mom, you have inspired me to be a strong woman, to speak up for myself, and to be fearless. You need a sort of confidence and strength to take on activism, and to handle the sad parts of it, too. I would not be the person that I am today without you and Dad. Thank you for always working so hard to learn about vegan food over the years, and I am grateful for all of the vegan holidays that you have hosted and for all of the plant-based foods that you've learned to make for me over the years! There's nothing greater than a mother's love.

Dad, thank you for helping me to see that animals are not food. I remember being a small child and noticing that you didn't want to eat meat that had bones or veins in it; that sparked a wise knowledge in me that has grown so much, and continues to do so. Thank you for encouraging me to learn more about the world and for passing on such a wonderful passion for education. It is because of you and your cooking style that being in the kitchen is fun and never feels like a job. I am so proud of you for becoming a vegetarian—though I am not surprised; you've always been a kind soul. Thanks to you and Mom, I am fulfilling and exceeding my fiercest dreams.

To my brother, L, for always being my biggest cheerleader. You have been so supportive of my vegan lifestyle and have gotten so involved in the cause. Thank you for always going out of your way to prepare vegan meals at your home, to order vegan foods at all the events you and your family host; you do it not because you have to, but because you have a truly beautiful heart. You are my BFF, and I'm always the most excited to tell *you* about my professional accomplishments; you are always so genuinely happy for me. Your faith and goodness inspires me to be a person of virtue, always. And thank you and Tammy for the delicious recipe and your contributions to this book!

To D and R, thank you for all of the support and encouragement, always. Lots of love and appreciation to you both.

Thank you to my friends, Jenn Mann and Eric Schiffer. You are such a lovely couple and truly wonderful people. Your activism and kindness is an inspiration to so many people. Thank you for your help and your contributions to this cookbook.

To the amazing folks at Hatherleigh Press: Andrew Flach, Ryan Tumambing, Anna Krusinski, Ryan Kennedy and the rest of the Hatherleigh family, thank you so much for all of your hard work and dedication. Thank you for believing in this project as much as I do and for sharing my vision for this book. You made this possible. Thank you for helping me to check off a dream from my list!

Most importantly, thank you to the animals: the "why I do what I do." I will never stop fighting for your freedom.

And thank you to the fans, readers, fellow activists and friends who have been working so bravely and selflessly to be voices for the animals. To my readers, especially those who have been reading my posts and articles since I first began writing, and have been asking for this cookbook for many years—this is for you!

Coffeehouse Style Pumpkin
Cream Cheese Muffins, page 59

Peanut Butter Tofu Stir-fry,
page 98

About the Author

Catherine Gill is a writer, blogger, and holistic vegan chef who specializes in natural and health foods. She studied and found her passion in writing, literature, and social science in college. She runs the popular blog The Dirty Vegan since 2010, focusing on comfort-food-style vegan recipes that are fun, accessible, and healthy. She also ran Dirty Vegan Foods, a vegan bakery specializing in veganized versions of classic desserts. She has an active social media presence with nearly 23,000 followers on Twitter (@TheDirtyVegan). She currently resides in New England with her husband, daughter, and rescue dog.

Split Pea Soup with Tempeh "Bacon",
page 106

Index of Recipes